Denis Newiak

PREPARING FOR THE GLOBAL BLACKOUT
A Disaster Guide from TV and Cinema

Denis Newiak

Preparing for the
Global Blackout

A Disaster Guide from TV and Cinema

Bibliographic information published by the Deutsche Nationalbibliothek

Die Deutsche Nationalbibliothek lists this publication in the Deutsche Nationalbibliografie; detailed bibliographic data are available in the Internet at http://dnb.d-nb.de.

Bibliografische Information der Deutschen Nationalbibliothek

Die Deutsche Nationalbibliothek verzeichnet diese Publikation in der Deutschen Nationalbibliografie; detaillierte bibliografische Daten sind im Internet über http://dnb.d-nb.de abrufbar.

Cover picture: © Agnormark | stock.adobe.com

ISBN-13: 978-3-8382-1661-4

© *ibidem*-Verlag, Stuttgart 2022

Printed in the United States of America

CONTENTS

This book was first published in German language as *Blackout – nichts geht mehr: Wie wir uns mit Filmen und TV-Serien auf einen Stromausfall vorbereiten können* (Marburg: Schüren) in June 2022.

Numbers indicate playing time in minutes.

Marginalia summarize the core statement of a paragraph.

THIS TIME, WE KNOW BETTER: LEARNING FROM CINEMATIC DISASTERS

Planes full of frightened passengers suddenly can no longer land normally because the pilots cannot find the runway after the airport lights failed, the entire country is in the dark. Doctors operate with flashlights and improvised cutlery in their completely overcrowded hospitals: since the emergency power has been cut, the number of victims from raging fires, diabetics suffering from insulin deficiency, and patients waiting for dialysis continues to grow. Not even the governmental radio communication is working anymore. Because you can no longer get on the Internet, you can only get information (if you still have one lying around) from the radio: the last stations with emergency power still report on where there is looting and rioting or where a nuclear power plant is about to meltdown (the reactor cooling has failed, because there is no more diesel). Those who want to communicate with each other need either radios or, those who can afford it, a satellite phone. Card payment terminals are out of service anyway, so if you need food or medicine, you pay for it with whatever you have on you, if necessary with your grandfather's gold watch to get a box of antibiotics. Because the hygienic conditions on the lower floors of high-rise buildings have become unacceptable (no one has been able to flush the toilet for a week), millions of people have to be relocated to stinking emergency shelters (the last wet wipes have long since been used up). If there were not this constant fear, since in the local prison the inmates used the opportunity to free themselves: now murderers and rapists are running around freely, and because police officers no longer come to work, no one will catch them anytime soon...

These scenes sound like something out of a movie or television, and that's what they are: highly speculative, dramatized and spectacularly staged – seemingly completely unrealistic, purely fictional, entertainment for an evening of horror that ends with everything being fine in reality, thankfully. But that's what we thought of pandemic movies like *Outbreak* and virus series like *The Rain* – until March 2020, when arenas became emergency hospitals, people in bright yellow protective suits buried hundreds of body bags in New York's Central Park, and conspiracy ideologues railed against vaccination. Suddenly, the television news and our everyday reality were filled with incubation periods and infection counts, social distancing and quarantine policies, personal tragedies and moments of hope when the antigen test comes back negative. *It's all been there before*, namely in popular culture and especially in feature films and television series: here, rapidly spreading viral illnesses were a standard motif long before the Corona pandemic, and reality caught up with it. Although researchers had warned of an impending pandemic for years, politicians and society were caught largely unprepared by the crisis, with the familiar terrible consequences: while some still indulge in the luxury of discussing mandatory vaccination instead of finally enacting it, two years into the pandemic, there are at least 6 million deaths worldwide, tens of millions of long-term damages, and hundreds of millions of children without orderly schooling – and the next variants are already waiting to strike immunologically naïve hosts.

Pandemics are a perfidious affair: they seemingly arise out of nowhere and appear as if out of the blue, while the dangerous viruses themselves are not directly perceptible and only indirectly reveal their dangerousness through the tragic consequences. It requires not only a great deal of self-discipline but also sound scientific knowledge to confront an invisible enemy like a plague, while denial of reality and recklessness can prove deadly. The last comparably fatal pandemic, which was caused by the HI virus and the immune deficiency AIDS, seems to have been largely forgotten, although a high six-digit number of people still die from the treacherous disease every year. Until 2020, pandemics were not part of our everyday perception, but rather a niche problem that experts in laboratories and clinics struggled with. At the very least, however, many people had already become acquainted with globally rampant pathogens through film and television, whether via genre classics such as *Contagion* or zombie series like *The Walking Dead*: here as there, humanity is fighting against a plague of immense proportions, while we as a cinema and TV audience are entertained by it (Newiak 2021). Then the Corona virus swept over us – and suddenly hand disinfection, N95 masks and death statistics were no longer movie props, but part of our everyday lives.

After a year of working on the topic of blackouts in movies and television, I feel like I'm caught in a never-ending déjà vu: the warnings are getting louder, that a widespread blackout could be one of the most significant risks for the next five to ten years, even more urgent than climate change. In film and television, blackouts have always been present anyway. Beyond cinematic pop culture, two books in particular have brought the issue to public attention in the past ten years. In 2010, the "Office of Technology Assessment at the German Bundestag" (TAB) published its final report on "Endangerment and Vulnerability of Modern Societies – Using the Example of a Large-Scale and Long-Lasting Power Supply Failure," commissioned by the Bundestag's Committee on Education, Research and Technology Assessment two years earlier. The official researchers came to the frightening conclusion that, in the event of an incident, "even after a few days, it is no longer possible to guarantee area-wide supplies of vital/necessary goods and services to meet with the public's requirements within the region affected by the blackout" (Petermann et al. 2011, 32). In sometimes disturbing detail, the experts describe the short-, medium- and long-term consequences of a blackout for politics, society, the economy and every individual, when the state can no longer fulfill "its duty of protection, as anchored in the Basic Law [the German Constitution], to protect the life and limb of its citizens" (Petermann et al. 2011, 32). The researchers show how in the case of a blackout, for example, the supply of food, medicines, and reliable information collapses, potentially leading to the loss of the state's monopoly on the use of force.

The study obviously served not only as a great inspiration for the novel *Blackout – Tomorrow Will Be Too Late* by Marc Elsberg, which was published in 2012 and still enjoys a large readership worldwide. Here, terrorists, driven by a crude ideological mix of hostility to civilization and a yearning for anarchy, destroy the power supply in Europe and the USA by hacking and manipulating the control elements of power plants – very much like the very real Stuxnet worm did in 2010, albeit with less fatal consequences than in the novel. In the book, one character feels remarkably reminiscent of the movie *Live Free or Die Hard* (USA 2007) with Bruce Willis, when someone claims that the issue of energy security is simply not yet present enough. Now, at least in fiction, the damage has been done, and "we've only ourselves to blame, because back then, everyone wrote off the dangers as so much craziness from doomsday prophets," as one of Elsberg's (2013, 117) character's exhorts. His main hero, the gifted computer scientist Monzano, sees the military driving through the streets and thinks to himself: "Like in a disaster movie"(Elsberg 2013, 236). Even in the highly acclaimed science fiction novel *2034 – A Novel of the Next World War* (Ackerman and Stavridis 2021), attacks on technical and electrical infrastructure are carried out to weaken the enemy militarily. After The White House's computers are infiltrated and undersea cables are destroyed, email accounts and cell phones no longer work, not even the candy machine does its job. *"This is bad, this is bad, this is bad,"* goes through a character's mind when nothing works anymore (Ackerman and Stavridis 2021, 49).

These dangers played out in fiction are not plucked out of thin air. In the event of a blackout, everything could quickly be at stake: our accustomed modern standard of living and the things we take for granted, such as running water, stable nutrition and health care – but also our concepts of security and order, which could no longer be fully guaranteed by an overstretched state, as well as our idea of solidarity, which is put to a severe test while any crises. The TAB study and many recent novels, but especially film and television, have recently brought remarkable attention to the subject. The current situation of the invasion of Russian troops into Ukraine and the discussion about missing gas supplies from Eastern Europe, but also the planned shutdown of nuclear power plants and missing power lines between North and South in Germany, the increasing grid complexity due to the desirable increase in renewable energies, dangerous electricity speculations in an over-liberalized market and near-collapses of the grid, awareness of possible operator errors, cyberterrorism and hacker attacks, but also recent natural disasters such as on the Rhine in July 2021 and during the hurricanes in February 2022 – all these recent events have catapulted the neglected problem of an impending blackout into the evening

news. While editorials, reports and essays are warning more and more perceptibly and seriously of the
growing danger of a blackout, the German tabloid
Bild-Zeitung, for example, criticized a public
television report for giving important tips on social
media on how to prepare for a widespread prolonged power blackout. *Westdeutscher Rundfunk*
recommended that people keep a basic supply of
food, drinking water, medicines and cash for 10
days, as well as flashlights and a radio, in order to
be able to bridge a supply gap self-sufficiently and
thus "relax into the blackout." With apocalyptic
panic imaginings – which of course would be caused
by the hated green energy turnaround – the right-
wing *Bild-Zeitung* accused *WDR* of 'trivializing'
such a crisis, instead of making clear that in fact with
comparatively little effort, as described by the public
broadcaster, major damage during such a catastrophe could easily be avoided. In fact, risk assessors
from TAB already showed ten years ago, with refer-
ence to previous studies, that the public is not prepared for a power blackout to any noticeable degree
[...] and people are therefore unable to cope adequately with the consequences" (Petermann et al.
2011, 231). On the other hand, anyone who warns
of the obvious immediate consequences of a blackout and wants to point out the lack of awareness of
it quickly finds themselves accused of either scare-
mongering or appeasement – but this does not make
things any better.

However, the lack of preparation for such a
scenario affects not only the civilian population, but

also society as a whole, including the authorities and institutions that are actually responsible for it. To date, as the German Federal Office of Civil Protection and Disaster Assistance (BBK) also concludes, "there is no national strategy in Germany that promotes comprehensive disaster risk management as a cross-cutting task," and thus no significant cross-state and cross-agency prevention against the disaster event of a blackout (BBK 2022; own translation). Germany is not alone in facing this problem: in hardly any European country – exceptions are perhaps Austria and Switzerland – has the topic of "blackout" been on the agenda so far. The consequences for practically all areas of society would be devastating: a widespread power blackout would cause damage worth billions of Euros within hours, grow into a national crisis within days, cause social life to collapse after just one week and could endanger democracies as a whole. This is not doom and gloom, but rather a scientifically proven, quite plausible and also probable matter against the background of expert discourse.

Pandemics, climate change, blackouts – all these crises were easily foreseeable and came with long advance warning from experts and popular culture alike. Hardly any catastrophe, however, was announced more carefully than the blackout. Scenarios of a widespread, prolonged power blackout are now almost part of everyday life in movies and on television, and they have become more widespread in recent years. Now we are waiting for it. But what exactly will happen when the time comes?

How do you think the people affected will behave? What effects will occur that could not have been predicted in academic papers? From a film and television studies perspective, the question then arises: What stories of the blackout do film and television tell? What images of the future, figuratively and literally, do these works create? And what insights can be derived from them that official recommendations cannot bring themselves to, that remain abstract and unapproachable in scientific description but become vivid and tangible in cinematic processing?

Few things are more strongly associated with modernity than electricity: power lines are the blood vessels of modern civilization, the current flowing through them the lifeblood of all modern facilities – from the water tap to the automated stock exchange to the Internet. With a widespread power outage, the entirety of modern life quickly threatens to fail. Today, virtually all technologies that enable and facilitate modern life – communications, health care, logistics – depend on electricity: When electricity is gone, toilets stop flushing, hospitals have to shut down after two days, traffic lights, milking systems and refrigerators fail. The loss of electricity is perhaps the only disaster that could challenge modernity as a whole. A blackout could not only temporarily disable modernization, but reverse it altogether. Film and television bear witness to this ever-present but publicly and politically underestimated danger: in a complex, increasingly globally interconnected 21st century world struggling with novel threat scenarios such as resource scarcity and terrorism, the likelihood of blackouts is increasing – as is their fatality. In the German feature film *The Coming Days* (*Die kommenden Tage,* D 2010), for example, mentally deranged globalization critics attack the power supply in order to force a violent coup – they use the blackout to destabilize an already battered society that has to wash its hair with water from a tetrapak. For the employees and patients of a hospital in Houston, Texas, the powerless *14 Hours* (USA 2005) becomes a nerve-racking ordeal after the emergency power system is flooded – although, as a result of climate change, extreme weather events must be expected more frequently in the future, the power grid as well as replacement systems need to be prepared for that. In a psychologically dense way, *Into the Forest* (CA 2015) shows how narrow the line is between electrified modernity and de-electrified post-modernity: even if food shortages can be bridged for a short time, at the latest at the moment of accident (such as an injury requiring treatment), danger (crime), or simply a lack of division of labor (in the end, the moldy house collapses), it becomes apparent how strongly we depend on functioning modern infrastructures and the observance of social roles and obligations, all of which ultimately depend on electricity (cf. fig. 1).

Figure 1: The small family of Into the Forest *(M04) is warned by radio shortly before the nationwide blackout – but by then it is too late to prepare adequately. Fortunately, the single father has some supplies, a power generator and battery-powered radio equipment in the secluded forest cottage. The moment when you have to rely on outside help (the police) and modern infrastructure (a hospital) becomes your undoing.*

Movies and series show that modern society as a whole, as well as individuals, are usually caught completely unprepared by the widespread power outage. The characters often still find a flashlight and a few candles – but the food, drinking water, and medicine reserves run out surprisingly quickly. Who has a supply these days, when you can easily buy everything you need for your daily needs in the supermarket or even have it delivered to your door? In blackout films and series, moments of surprising helpfulness and solidarity often arise out of necessity. In hospital series like *Grey's Anatomy* (USA 2005–), for example, medical staff perform emergency surgery on their patients in stuck elevators until they are totally exhausted. The firefighters of *Chicago Fire* (USA 2012–) fight against carbon monoxide poisoning, because some freezing citizens have tried to warm up at the fireplace without airing their room. In sitcoms – whether *Friends* (USA 1994–2004), *The Big Bang Theory* (USA 2007–2019) or *Family Matters* (USA 1989–1998) – neighbors and family members who previously lived anonymously next door to each other encounter each other anew as they help and keep each other company in times of need, sometimes bringing them closer together again than they would have thought possible. And in crime series and thrillers, such as *Bones* (USA 2005–2017) or *Designated Survivor* (USA 2016–2019), a blackout initially makes work more difficult, but also produces innovative ideas and creative solutions that would never have come to mind under normal circumstances.

But when sooner or later there is a lack of necessities, fictional characters quickly tend toward irrational behavior that is overridden by the instinct for self-preservation. When push comes to shove, in fiction every individual is out for his or her own. In the French series *L'Effondrement* ("The Collapse" FR 2019), inspired by collapsology, for example, people fight for every morsel and last drop of fuel they can still get in a world where energy supplies have completely collapsed due to shortages – although the modern world was clearly warned, here it is running into the open knife (as in the case of the pandemic). Even the last characters who stand up for others in the midst of hopelessness feel compelled to give up sooner or later, such as the self-sacrificing caretaker of an old people's home: at the end, he tearfully euthanizes the starving and pain-stricken residents.

If blackout films and series have one thing in common, it is the shared awareness that precautions are comparatively easy to take, on both a small and a large scale, at least in relation to the potentially serious damage that can occur: each individual can easily make preparations to better withstand a widespread blackout with an adequate supply of food, water and medicines, a battery-powered radio, a portable charger, and a camping stove. But governments and businesses also need to take greater precautions – ministries and hospitals as well as nuclear power plants – to prevent catastrophic chain reactions. In addition to large reserves of food, fuel, and emergency generators, what is needed above all is greater risk sensitivity and innovative concepts, not least in view of the growing challenges posed by the more complex grid structure as a result of the energy transition as well as the imminent dangers posed by hacker attacks on utilities and infrastructures. In the German TV series *Blackout* (D 2021), for example, not only the control instruments of power plants but also the supposedly 'smart' digital electricity meters in individual households are attacked en masse in order to set domino effects in motion that lead to the collapse of the European power grid – and thus to the collapse of the entire social life, paid for with thousands of victims.

How can one prepare today – as an individual as well as a state – for such a situation, which hopefully will never occur, but which nevertheless cannot be ruled out and is potentially devastating if it does happen? There are various ways of acquiring the necessary knowledge to act. One can read professional articles and scientific papers, but academic studies, with few exceptions, have the unfortunate feature of being cryptic to a non-specialist audience. Their findings may be empirically validated, but they remain inaccessible, technical and abstract, and are therefore not particularly helpful to individuals when it comes to concrete action – which is not a problem, because that is not their purpose either, as they are meant to advance scientific discourse for a highly qualified audience. Of course, you can consult one of the thousands of guidebooks, but many of these guides are quite bold and speculative, occasionally quite tendentious, and sometimes overtly interest-driven – sometimes even propagating conspiracy theories. Some books, which actively address the so-called "prepper" and "survivalism" scene (for whose followers crisis preparedness becomes the most important purpose in life), seem to literally wish for the social decline, as probably some of their readers do, in order to reset liberal democracy in the moment of weakness and to install a power order according to their own anti-democratic ideas. Of course, you can also trust the videos of missionary "Youtubers" – they seem to know exactly what they are talking about, right? The commitment of the many, often unpaid informing video makers must be appreciated, but among them, as among the "influencers" in so-called "social networks," there are many charlatans: they tend to overdramatize their stories for selfish interests, hoping that you click on their links to emergency generators, water canisters and silver coins, through which the self-proclaimed enlighteners receive not insignificant commissions. The more people are afraid of such a video and click there, the more can be earned with the blackout, even before it has taken place.

In comparison, the cinematic art forms of cinema and television series appear much more illustrative, informative, and trustworthy. Of course, they don't exist simply out of goodwill either: they primarily want to attract our attention in order to tie us to a streaming platform, increase viewer ratings, or justify the investment of a movie ticket – which is justified given the immense costs and creative work behind every film and TV series. The great advantage of fictional cinematic art forms is that they hardly have to obey any rules and can develop freely in terms of design and content: film and series makers can choose the themes and motifs that they believe will achieve the greatest audience success, which leads screenwriters, directors and popular actors to turn to those subjects that affect the audience. The fictional world should have something to do with our own hopes and desires as well as fears and worries about the future, so that we can identify with the story and make it meaningful to us. In this way, films and television series expose, in Angela

Keppler's sense, "what is *relevant in* different areas of society, what matters in politics and economics, culture and art, science and lifestyle" (Keppler 2006, 317; own translation).

Wolfgang Bonß had described that modernity tends to "exponentially increasing, industrially generated catastrophic potentials" (Bonß 1995, 11; own translation), since "the growing possibilities have to be bought with an unintended increase of uncertainty and ambiguity" (Bonß 1995, 22; own translation). To put it in one sentence: the comfortable, dynamic, and stimulating life in the globalized late modern age can probably only be had if one is willing to accept an airplane crash, a pandemic, or a nuclear meltdown now and then. In spite of the drastic experiences that such catastrophes entail (not only those directly affected, but also through public reporting), they do not become part of everyday perception as exceptional situations of civilization. At the same time, individual psychological processes force a temporary repression of the omnipresent dangers, since a domestication of modernity would not be possible at all under constant feelings of fear. While we, as risk sociologist Ulrich Beck puts it, live through and suffer the everyday experiences of this increasingly threatening modernity with "its turmoils, contradictions, symbols, ambivalences, fears, ironies, and hidden hopes [...] without grasping them and without understanding them" (Beck 2007, 19; own translation), films and television series about catastrophes and crises allow us to deal with these dangers without damage in order to react appropriately in the event of an incident.

Severe accidents, fires, storms, and hazardous substance releases can unleash the potential to make parts of modernity uninhabitable or unlivable, which is why modern society must have an interest in also being able to deal with the exceptional situation of disaster. Because catastrophes that are potentially associated with great damage have not yet occurred naturally, and therefore do not reveal themselves of their own accord in the present with their possible causes and consequences, a modern society must first develop an awareness of future dangers in order to be able to avert them in advance, to control them by prophylaxis in the event of damage, or, if nothing else helps, at least to get through them alive. A naïve modernity that is caught off guard by its inherent forces of destruction can, in the worst case, turn into its opposite. Blackout films and series conspicuously prefer narratives that show a modernity struggling to survive the widespread blackout (for example, in the Belgian series *Black-Out*, 2020–2021), or that unwind the de-electrified society directly into a *pre*-modernity (for example, in *Fear The Walking Dead*, USA 2015 –, or in *Tribes of Europa*, D 2021).

By bringing dangers such as a blackout 'into the present,' films and television series achieve by means of their fictional liberties what Beck calls the "*reality staging of* world risk": "For it is only through the visualization, the staging of world risk, that the future of the catastrophe becomes present –

often with the aim of averting it by influencing present decisions." (Beck 2007, 30; own translation) For Eva Horn, this is the special quality of cinematic fictions of catastrophe, because they "seem to depict something that we consider possible and perhaps even imminent, but at the same time cannot imagine, cannot grasp" (Horn 2014, 21; own translation). For Elena Esposito, it is precisely in this fictionalization of possible futures that a particularly dense experience of reality emerges – denser than immediately perceptible social reality can ever achieve:

> *Fiction allows for the portrayal of deception, intrigue, or observational relationships that cannot be observed in actual reality, which is rarely realistic. Consequently, those who are able to engage with these features of fictional texts are better able to navigate the real world and the complexities of its relationships.* (Esposito 2014, 56; own translation)

Modernity, according to Esposito, is characterized by the fact that "real reality is becoming increasingly opaque," i.e., it is more and more escaping immediate perception due to a rapid pace of change, complex interdependencies, and a high degree of mechanization (Esposito 2014, 199). At the same time reasonable decisions in the present determine whether the future unfolds as a space for shaping or closes itself off as a zone of danger. This is why procedures through which one can gain access to reality and thus also to possible futures are becoming essential for the survival of modern society. Whereas until recently 'the fronts' were clearly settled – just think of the division of the world into two hostile camps until 1990 – the high degree of abstraction of present-day dangers (cyberterrorism initiated from afar, the multiplication of conspiracy ideologies, disruptive events arising from cascading effects, etc.), according to Slavoj Žižek, brings the problem that we as modern people can no longer directly confront the uncertainties arising from them: we cannot look the causative sources in the eye due to their opacity (Žižek 2011, 360). Disaster films and series, on the other hand, cast their 'spotlights' on otherwise hidden discourses, such as unjust relations of "class, race and gender" (Keane 2006, 74), which in the light of artistic engagement emerge as directly visible figures in their own right – for example, in the form of cinematic characters in whose position viewers can put themselves and whose decision-making dilemmas can be comprehended.

Keppler is convinced that television in particular – "[i]n its continuous articulation and variation of what the current landmarks of what is real and important are" – is what enables modern society to develop "a collective consciousness of the present" in the first place (Keppler 2006, 317; own translation), and thus also of the catastrophic potentials smoldering within it. For Marcus Kleiner, the accompanying strong media presence of crises is "a traditional way of coping with crises that lends a higher teleological sense to the experience of uncertainty and threat" (Kleiner 2013, 228; own translation), i.e., conveys the feeling that the dangers and risks confronting us are not random and thus uncontrollable, but a logical consequence of the process of modernization – if not preventable, maybe at least containable. Kay Kirchmann describes for television how, through "the *reflexive thematization of alternative selection options in the narrative process itself,*" it is capable of producing "alternative and at the same time antinomic plot designs within *one* narrative" (Kirchmann 2006, 163; own translation): through the "subjunctive narrative forms" specific to television series (Kirchmann 2006, 167), in the media view, the possibility arises to take a look at different possible courses of events and to observe how decisions in the narrated present within the fictional logic affect the future of the plot, whether they lead to desirable and undesirable consequences.

As can be seen here, film and television research consistently sees a high importance of its objects of study in the participation in socially relevant processes of creating and conveying meaning, especially in the context of future issues and crises (cf. chapter 1). Against this background, it is also not surprising that films and television series are being taken up in a conspicuous manner more and more frequently in specialist and non-fiction books, but also in press reporting, in order to activate the assumed pop-cultural knowledge of the readership, listeners, and viewers and to profit from the familiarity and appeal of such works by allowing their glamor to radiate onto their own presentation. How often have we heard in recent years, for example in the context of the Corona pandemic, that we would see 'pictures like from a science fiction film'? In this way, authors and journalists prove that the otherwise elusive discourses of scientific problems become more comprehensible and tangible with the help of cinematic fictions. In most of these cases, however, there is no real interest in the filmic works themselves as a form of expression; rather, the series and movies on which they focus often serve only as cues and have to serve as illustrations of a complex context that would otherwise have to be skillfully and elaborately formulated or illustrated by the authors themselves. The sophisticated cinematic forms of expression then threaten to become banal decals of a certain idea of 'social reality,' which become more easily recognizable in the 'mirror' of the medium, but in fact only conceal the construct character of such presuppositions.

However, this book is not about explaining the problem of blackouts on the basis of movies and TV series, anecdotally stringing scenes together to misuse them as evidence of the 'real' danger of blackouts. Rather, we want to let the films and television series speak for themselves: What imaginaries of blackout do such works develop? Which narratives dominate the blackout scenarios and which ones stand out in particular? What forms of staging appear in such works and in what light do they cast the problem of the blackout? And how do the fictions position themselves in relation to the objectively real danger of a widespread blackout? What have the artworks "thought of" that is not even "on our radar" yet? Needless to say, feature films and television series are subject to a different logic, a particular form of knowledge order, than scientific discourse or everyday language arguments: cinematic art forms are not primarily concerned with whether we, as viewers, perceive the scenarios they show as warnings of a future risk that is relevant to society as a whole, or whether we can even read out courses of action that help us deal with them. It is not part of the production intention of cinematic art forms to serve the audience something extraneous (didactic, alarming, prophetic) on a silver platter – strictly speaking, they don't want *anything* for themselves. Certainly, one may also assume that the production collectives and the individuals acting in them have certain interests, ideas, perhaps also some idealism and missionary aims that crawl into the finished work. However, since the creators of such works are themselves part of the social totality and do not move in a hermetically sealed special sphere, but rather are forced to respond to the (actual and assumed) wishes, needs and hopes of the audience in order to generate a large viewership, it is unlikely that problematic systematic errors, denials of reality, or attempts at manipulation will take root in a collectively produced film or television series. Rather, a society generates precisely those films and television series that must emerge from it at a certain point in time; they then appear as a mosaic of the countless fragments of discourse that circulate in the fast-moving late-modern social present.

Of course, standard film and television research methods, even the elaborate experimental setups of media psychology, do not allow us to make any firm statements about a concrete "learning effect" on individuals from watching a series or a film – the interplay between a consciousness that cannot be directly observed and an aesthetically complex play with images and sound is too dynamic, interdependent, and ultimately inscrutable for that. Because individuals naturally derive their knowledge of the world not only from film and television, but from upbringing in family, school, and clubs, through peer groups and special caregivers, other mass media, and direct experience in dealing with the environment, it is difficult, perhaps impossible, to neatly separate these various fragments. However, it seems not only intuitive but also plausible to assume that films and television series make a considerable contribution to the transmission of knowledge, which is then circulated and made usable in a society. Ultimately, maybe it is not important to be able to say that a certain person has acquired flashlights, camping stoves, and emergency supplies just because he or she was shown doing so in a film or television series (even if, I may say with certainty, this is true at least for myself). What seems decisive for the context underlying this book is that popular art forms, and above all cinematic forms of expression, can contribute to sensitizing people to certain trends and constellations that are just becoming relevant, but still have to mature in discourse before they are ready to be spoken about. Feature films and series share with each other, but with no other art form or mass medium, the unique property of making highly complex social contexts immediately perceptible to the senses with a forceful vividness. At the same time, they are creating a strong affectation, an individual empathic connection between what is shown and what is viewed, thereby lending the fictional universes into which such works draw us a special *probability,* which is what makes the reception of such works so appealing in the first place: they cause a flood of plausible images of the social, allowing us to better explain to ourselves and each other the reality of our own lives that we inhabit beyond cinematic fiction, to better settle into everyday reality by making appropriate choices, and to interact meaningfully with each other.

It seems plausible that the population also orientates itself to fictions in order to take knowledge from them for their own everyday life and also for crisis situations. Knut Hickethier, for example, sees television as an important "part of the social modernization processes" (Hickethier 1994, 70; own translation), which has the task of "enabling individuals [...] to live within society, because competent individuals are necessary for the continued existence of a complex society" (Hickethier 2008, 47; own translation). In view of the constantly changing challenges that the high pace of modernization poses to individual members of society, macro-socially effective institutions are needed to prepare individuals for coping with new life situations and thus also for dealing appropriately with a catastrophe, thus keeping modern society functioning. To this end, television series undertake "a permanent behavioral modeling of the participants" (ibid.) so that the individual members of society do not fail in the increasingly complex modern everyday life. In this light, the fictional play with crises and catastrophes that can be read as a rupture of modernization appears as a risk-free social experiment, because, according to Horn, cinematic catastrophes bring into focus "what cannot be seen in the space of intact civilization, reliable supply, and functioning infrastructures: the catastrophic fitness of society and its institutions" (Horn 2014, 191; own translation). Films and television series that address crisis situations such as a blackout can, on the one hand, point to possible breaking points in society by showing the limits of the disaster fitness of the acting characters; on the other hand, approaches unfold in the narratives as to how such a crisis could be dealt with appropriately – even if it is only that one thinks at the end of the film or series that one will do things *quite differently* oneself than the characters who failed in the fiction.

This book is dedicated to the decoding of this implicit knowledge inscribed in cinematic art forms on the subject of blackout. In doing so, it is also my hope that by making explicit the creative behavioral and problem-solving knowledge hidden in film and television, it will enable those who otherwise do not have or find access to film and television, or who have special responsibilities in crisis preparedness and management, to behave appropriately in a crisis. Therefore, like the comparable volume on pandemic films published by Schüren-Verlag in 2020 (translation by ibidem-Verlag in 2021), this book is aimed not only at a readership with an affinity for film and television who want to get to know their favorite flicks and series once again from a new perspective, but also at those in positions of responsibility in politics, administration and business, for whom creative ideas for dealing with the disaster potentials of the 21st century are unlikely to do any harm in view of the changing threat situations. The elegant thing about film and television remains that they merely make suggestions that the audience can accept or reject, and that the works of art are quite indifferent to whether we can gain something from their offers of meaning and behavior – or let the opportunity pass by. It remains the decision of the individual whether we simply let the catastrophe of the blackout – like the pandemic – come upon us again (and are then overrun by it defenselessly), or whether we still use the preparation time now to stand there wiser this time. There is still time, but it is unclear how long we have left.

Denis Newiak
Potsdam, Germany, June 2022

Translated in July 2021

1. BLACKOUT EVERYWHERE: ON THE OMNIPRESENCE OF A FRAGILE MODERNITY

In the rich industrialized regions of the world, we have long since become accustomed to the fact that the goods of daily life are constantly available. The supermarket shelves are full, pharmacies and doctors provide reliable help in the event of illness, and the gas pumps run uninterrupted. Even though many things have recently become more expensive and there were temporary fears of supply bottlenecks due to the Covid-19 crisis, modern consumer society has proven to be surprisingly resilient. The situation is similar with the availability of electricity: hardly anything is taken more for granted than electricity, which has to come out of the socket like a human right guaranteed for eternity. One reason why we simply accept this is that electricity is almost always there, because power outages have long since ceased to be an everyday occurrence in this country: every year, German households, for example, experience supply gaps of a good quarter of an hour, mostly unnoticed at night. Accordingly, it is not surprising that there has long been little awareness of the danger of a prolonged and widespread power blackout, either among the population or in politics; the idea that the electrified society would have to live without televisions and smartphones, electric heaters and refrigerators, ventilators and ATMs, even temporarily, seems too absurd. The very idea arouses nightmares.

In modern society hardly any gaps in supply – power outages rare

In recent years, however, the blackout has had an astonishing career in public discourse. Until recently, it was regarded primarily as a purely technical problem with a low probability of occurrence, which at most had to be dealt with by the employees (who always had to consider the worst case scenario) in the control centers of large energy suppliers. In the meantime, the blackout is increasingly perceived by a broader public as a real potential danger, which continues to build up, especially due to the necessary but not unproblematic changes in the energy industry and infrastructure (cf. chapter 2). In recent months in particular, crisis and catastrophe rhetoric has soared to unprecedented heights: threats of power plant outages due to excessive Covid-19 sickness rates, rising energy prices, and most recently, of course, the Russian military's invasion of Ukraine along with the threat of missing gas deliveries and possible cyberattacks have unmasked the hitherto taken-for-granted, constantly functioning energy supply as fragile. Even comparatively small disruptions and manipulations could set off chain reactions that would be almost impossible to predict and then to influence – with the consequence of a widespread and prolonged collapse of the power supply that could endanger the modern way of life as a whole.

Blackout is increasingly recognized as a danger due to crises

The blackout thus appears to be a prime example of an internal contradiction typical of modern society: life today is *safer and more dangerous* than ever before. Despite all the injustices, backwardness and other deficits that

Benefits of comfortable and safe modern life are now taken for granted

continue to exist, life has never been more comfortable, safe and stimulating than in modern times – and at the same time we pay for this way of life by accepting ever new risks. Even if the individual modern human being is not always aware of it, a considerable part of the attractiveness that the modern world exerts on us comes from the comfortable living conditions – a stable food supply, increasingly homelike shelter and advanced medicine. Anyone who is too quick to assume that these achievements are secure for all eternity should take a brief look at 'pre-modern' times: just two hundred years ago, Europe was still dominated by the poorest conditions with an average life expectancy of less than 30 years, illiteracy and a rigid system of estates without any social mobility or welfare claims, whereas modern man enjoys ever new technical wonders, inalienable rights of freedom and the privilege of no longer having to worry seriously about the most existential questions of life.

Without closing our eyes to current challenges with it, it may be worthwhile to occasionally recall these achievements and the price we pay for them – after all, modern progress does not come free of charge: the highly efficient mode of production and the social processes trimmed for frictionless acceleration provoke overwork, excessive demands and loneliness. However, the longing for a more communal pre-modern way of life is then, after all, usually smaller than the cherished three safe meals, freedom from arbitrary exercise of power and running drinking water from the tap. Of course, the

The comfort of modernity has its price – but we can no longer live without it

constant availability of electricity and electronic devices – from the washing machine and the automobile to the most faithful companion of late-modern man: the cell phone – are also part of these practiced modern self-evident things. Once you get to know life in the modern age, you will hardly want to give it up.

Of course, modernity does not uneventfully follow a linear course. On the contrary, catastrophes are a typical part of modernity, they are, strictly speaking, a logical consequence of the achievements of modernization. If anyone can become an enemy of modernity, according to the risk researcher Ulrich Beck, then it is only modernity itself, because with all its desirable successes it also produces risks that turn against the achievements themselves (Beck 2007, 376): for airplane crashes and train accidents it first needs airplanes and trains, for reactor accidents and chemical accidents nuclear power plants and industry. Nevertheless, hardly anyone would think of stopping air traffic or banning plastic products because of the occasional fatal accident: because the advantages outweigh the disadvantages, the catastrophes of modernity are accepted. In view of the great victims and the indescribable suffering of such disasters, this sounds inconceivably heartless, but: modern people accept their disasters as collateral damage of the successes of modernization.

Modernity tends to catastrophes, which must be accepted for the sake of modernity's advantages

For Beck (2007, 394–402), the monstrous human catastrophes of the 20th century – world wars and the atomic bomb, the Holocaust and suicide bombings – can only be understood as typically modern phenomena because they, like all desirable aspects of modern life, are also fed by the logic of modernization with constantly growing and not always controllable technical, economic and scientific innovations. While catastrophic experiences did not play a central role in the post-war period, which was spoiled by consumption, Beck published his diagnosis of a *risk society* in 1986 under the impression of the Chernobyl accident: the devastating accident in the Soviet nuclear power plant would, as a "portent of a *modern middle age of danger*," from now on nourish an "*'ascriptive' fate of danger*" (Beck [1986] 2020, 8; own translation) that is inescapable for modern man, or to put it more simply: "Fear determines the attitude toward life." (Beck 2007, 28; own translation). To live under highly modernized conditions means having to enjoy the comfort of modernization's successes in constant awareness of impending catastrophe, of partial or complete doom.

Beck: For modern people, fear is becoming an unavoidable part of life

Whereas in the pre-modern era the fate of the world was in the hands of supernatural (heavenly) powers and one could only counter one's own powerlessness by believing in the good, the sciences, which developed with modernization, initially arouse the hope and also the desire to make things around us controllable: laws of nature suggest making the world predictable, so that by making

Modern rationality assumes that the world would be predictable and that harm could be avoided by reasonable decisions

conscious choices we can anticipate potential risks and thereby avoid harm before it occurs. Every person consciously and unconsciously makes such impact assessments every day, whether deciding for or against driving to work or attending a mass event when there is a high risk of infection. Even if exceptions confirm the rule, modern man is driven by a program of rationality to make the most reasonable decisions possible with a desirable outcome.

Modernity as a whole is also constantly making such trade-offs, and to do so it depends on turning to the future and mentally anticipating damage that may occur in order to avert it in the present with foresight. In relatively well-defined systems, the construction of causal relationships, i.e., statements about the probable relationship between causes and consequences, allows us to make justified assumptions about potential risk reductions: traffic rules and airbags clearly reduce risks of serious injury accidents, just as filter masks and vaccinations can contain viral diseases. The constantly nagging "fear that things could go wrong" is automatically part of modern everyday experience (Luhmann 1991, 6; own translation), but at the same time there remains the feeling that one's own actions can positively influence the conditions immediately around one, that one can make a difference.

Construction of causalities in undercomplex, clearly defined systems possible

Modern societies, however, tend toward a constant increase in their complexity, as a result of which it is not always possible to identify specific connections between cause and effect, and especially not for longer periods of time: Luhmann

Luhmann: In complex systems, causal relations can hardly be described anymore

(1991, 35) says that in modern societies "there are conditions that can trigger considerable damage without being attributable to decision, although it is clear that without decisions such damage could not have occurred," or as Beck already put it: "The highly differentiated division of labor corresponds to a general complicity and to this a general irresponsibility. Everyone is cause *and* effect and thus *non-cause*. Causes cloak themselves in a general variability of actors and conditions, reactions and counter-reactions." (Beck [1986] 2020, 43; own translation)

Under such conditions of increasing and at the same time opaque social dependency relationships, in which individual events can entail unimagined chains of consequences, a feeling can arise that "the *idea* guiding modernity of the controllability of decision-related side-effects and dangers has become questionable" (Beck 2007, 39–40; own translation), which can paralyze the handling of risks: after all, we apparently not only cannot foresee the impending catastrophes of the future, but also can hardly do anything about them. Modern man is thus plagued by "an incalculable unease as to whether, under these conditions of chronic uncertainty, the system of social dependence, despite all apparent stability, might not collapse at the moment of weakness in the form of a social catastrophe, whether a social existence under these conditions of structural uncertainty could be planned at all and thus lived through" (Newiak 2022a, 176; own translation).

> Highly complex present appears increasingly fragile and uncontrollable

However, if one were to make oneself comfortable in such a fatalistic basic attitude, the last days of modern society would be at hand, because: "Normal catastrophes can be compensated for, but the greatest possible catastrophes cannot. They *must* be prevented." (Beck 2007, 217; own translation) Obviously, there are conceivable catastrophes whose consequences could no longer be managed by appropriate means or perhaps not at all, be it a nuclear war, impending climate tipping points – or a long-lasting widespread power blackout. Whether such an avoidance of existentially decisive future dangers will still be possible with the present methods of "foresight and risk assessment" (Akremi 2011, 610; own translation) remains to be seen. The fact is that the modern age, organized on the basis of the division of labor, is skilled and highly efficient in handling manageable and acute problems, but "it is overburdened with the solution of fundamental challenges, because in this respect the scheme of differentiation stands in its way" (Nassehi 2021, 310; own translation): everyone is an expert in his or her special field, but hardly anyone has an eye for the big picture.

> Greatest possible catastrophes must be prevented because they threaten modernity as a whole

Nowhere is this more evident than in the face of impending eco-collapse. Because modern society lacks "internal stopping rules" (Nassehi 2021, 211; own translation), the tirades of destruction continue to escalate because there is as yet no functional mechanism of intervention. As the recently deceased socially engaged astrophysicist Stephen Hawking put it succinctly: "We have given our planet the

> Climate disaster like blackout could completely challenge modern way of life

catastrophic gift of climate change. Rising temperatures, retreating polar ice caps, forest dieback, overpopulation, diseases, war, famine, water shortages and the decimation of animal species – actually all solvable problems, but all of which have not been mastered to date." (Hawking 2020, 171; own translation) The destructive forces that can be dangerous to modernity as a whole are thus today primarily "'natural' catastrophes that are in fact man-made" (Beck 2017, 253; own translation). Climate change, it is becoming increasingly clear, is one of the few conceivable disasters that could completely engulf modernity, but it is also not the only one, and there are likely to be more rather than fewer in the foreseeable future. One of them is the threat of a widespread and prolonged power blackout, which after a certain period of time can hardly be brought under control.

According to Nassehi, we have long been in a "permanent crisis mode" in the face of these impending doomsdays, which on the one hand generates a high degree of problem-solving efficiency, but on the other hand entails "unavoidable excessive demands" (Nassehi 2021, 301; own translation). This excessive demand arises not least because the struggle against the catastrophic potentials of modernity sometimes feels like a battle against invisible windmills: whereas in pre-modern times the risks of life in the form of impending famine or untreatable diseases were constantly present, modernity has concealed the catastrophic potentials it has itself generated – with the con-

Catastrophes are suppressed or are not sufficiently noticeable in consequences, hence hardly any awareness

sequence that it is 'easier' to live, but at the same time the catastrophes, when they occur, strike individuals who are largely unprepared. The same is true of the climate crisis, which is already having a noticeable impact, but whose consequences are still too 'mild' (at least in the regions that are causing and at the same time less affected by it) for there to be any immediate pressure to suffer and act. The same applies to other impending future dangers and challenges that modern people will be confronted with sooner or later, be it dealing with increasingly powerful artificial intelligences, conspiracy ideologies that endanger social cohesion – or the risk of a blackout.

It is precisely the most serious potential dangers that are hardly noticeable in everyday experience: precisely because of their potentially stressful consequences, they are part of the social sub-conscious, but we are unable to address them directly. However, repression of unpleasant aspects of life is not only a potentially pathogenic thing in terms of individual psychology: just as therapy can help to deal with trauma through repressed memories and thus combat psychological suffering, a society is also well advised to deal with the catastrophic potentials smoldering in them. This can help not to be overwhelmed by them when things do get serious, and at the same time to be able to adopt a healthier basic attitude to the modern way of life, which is precisely not delivered with a guarantee of eternity.

Becoming aware of potential hazards in order to prepare for risks

Modernity, however, does not seem to have developed a healthy way of dealing with its catastrophes. It is true that, according to Nassehi, modernity invented "grand narratives" in response to the otherwise threatening feeling of power-lessness, "in order to come to terms with its own experiences of the disparate, of the crisis-like, of self-insecurity" – be it the narrative of the gift of reason, of freedom, or of the nation (Nassehi 2021, 33; own translation). Ultimately, however, it is precisely in light of these liberal constructions that modern societies shy away from imposing on individuals exuberant prescriptions about exactly how they should behave. Rather, (at least Western) modern societies relied on the "invention of the individual, who may and must now find his or her own way in the various demands of society" (Nassehi 2021, 151). This is not just an abstract philosophical idea, but is also reflected, for example, in basic assumptions of disaster manage-ment, which instead of complete state crisis pre-vention relies primarily on increasing individual resilience, i.e., the ability to help oneself when a catastrophe like a blackout hits society.

> In modern times, individuals are left to deal with disasters on their own – but how should they act?

Thus, every individual today is ultimately thrown back on him/herself when it comes to making decisions, be it in everyday life or in a disaster situation. It is hardly deniable that any modern society – for all its love of the idea of the self-determined subject – is dependent on a mini-mum social consensus about appropriate and in-appropriate behavior: only those who can rely on their fellow human beings not acting arbitrarily and not

> Modern life also requires minimal consensus on appropriate behavior, but is in a constant state of change

always differently in comparable situations can establish trust with others, which makes social interaction possible in the first place. This unwritten contract, however, is not set in stone due to the high pace of modernization: role concepts, professional requirements and ethical norms change in parallel and often unnoticed to social, scientific-technological and economic developments. How can modernity and its inhabitants keep pace with the high pressure of change? And at the same time, how can we ensure that modern people still behave appropriately in exceptional situations that deviate from everyday life?

Even if the interrelationships of the social transmission of meaning are highly complex and ultimately not really transparent, it is undisputed that – in addition to the classic socialization instances such as families and peer groups, schools and work environments – especially today the mass media have a considerable share in how we explain the world and its underlying rules to one another. Cinematic forms of art and expression are of particular importance in this regard. Hartley, for example, attributes to television similar functions of macrosocial communication as were organized in pre-modern times by church, family, and military (Hartley 1999, 38). Television, according to Gross and Morgan (1985, 222), would occupy a special role in the production of meaning, as the vivid recurring images of characters interacting socially against modern backdrops "share with virtually all members of society common cultural norms".

Social sensemaking through mass media, especially film and television series

Despite the apparent competition with other mass media phenomena such as "Social Media" (in which predominantly stereotypes and intrinsically meaningless fragments of everyday life are juxtaposed), the importance of film and television as society's 'meaning machines' has recently only increased. In particular, new types of television series, such as those found especially among the new big streaming providers, "allow us to meet the challenges of modernity and to master its errors without questioning its obvious successes: a free, comfortable, progressive life" (Newiak 2022b, 248), for instance by addressing otherwise tabooed social problems that only in the creative freedom of cinematic art forms physically confront us and thus become discursively 'tangible'.

Against this background, it is not surprising that films and television series deal so extensively with questions of the future and thus also with potential future dangers; one need only think of the great variety of science fiction films that deal with stark climate changes and extreme weather events, uncontrollable artificial intelligences and automated warfare, the threat of an impact by celestial bodies or devastating pandemics. Time and again, future films and series tell of catastrophic events that throw modernity off course or deal it the final decisive blow. But precisely because serious accidents, storms and fatal individual events, as exceptional situations, have no presence in everyday life and, as potential dangers of the future, have not yet occurred and are therefore not observable, the

> Future fictions reliably warn of neglected dangers – and thus allow prevention

narratives of impending catastrophes are of such great importance for society as a whole: "They are stories that are designed as *'cautionary tales'*. They tell of early indications of danger that are not taken seriously or not interpreted correctly" (Horn 2014, 284; own translation) – again and again with comparable consequences: an insufficiently resilient modernity is blindsided by an unforeseen or ignored hazard event, which not infrequently results in the decline of modernity, that is, in a 'post-modernity' – to be understood literally as an era 'after' modernity ends. For Horn, cinematic *"imaginative procedures of foresight"* thus fulfill an important function, "precisely to bring improbable disasters – such as the worst-case scenario or the 'chain of unfortunate circumstances' – into view" (Horn 2014, 303; own translation), so that appropriate precautions can be taken in the real world. The fact that these cinematic scenarios are fictional worlds does not do any harm; on the contrary, it is precisely in the aesthetic play with probabilities and ignorance that potential dangers can be worked out much more freely and sometimes more accurately than in the narrow corset of political, scientific, and economic discourse.

Certainly, it can be feared that cinematic end-of-world fictions play into the hands of an unhealthy pessimism; after all, apocalypses have something inevitable and thus unavoidable about them: "The scope of the present thus becomes ever narrower and shortens to the moment before the end." (Bahr 2001, 10; own translation) At the same

> Disaster films give meaning to impending crises and thus incentive to intervene

time, however, the media presence of end-time scenarios can be understood as "a traditional way of coping with crises" that "lends the experience of uncertainty and threat a higher teleological meaning" (Kleiner 2013, 228), thus making the impending catastrophes clear not as random and senseless, but as a logical consequence of the modern way of life. Only through this would forces be unleashed to be able to stop the impending end of the world after all – instead of surrendering to them.

However, cinematic doomsday fictions have had a remarkable, sometimes depressing career. For Hans Krah, doomsday fictions in the 21st century are no longer innocent mind games as metaphors for extraneous macro-social problems (think of green Martians who repeatedly had to invade the USA during the Cold War on behalf of the Soviets), but rather cinematic apocalypses today are "rationally derivable from general cultural knowledge" (Krah 2004, 16; own translation). At the latest since the experience of 9/11, catastrophes that would have been unthinkable only a short time before have not only advanced into the realm of the possible, but have in part already actually materialized; one need only think of the resurgence of the Cold War or the escalation of the climate issue: "[A]n extraordinary social and psychological change is taking place right in front of our eyes – the impossible is becoming possible. [...] [W]e *know* the (ecological) catastrophe is possible, probable even, yet we do not *believe* it will really happen." (Žižek 2011, 328) Thus, the tendency of the cinematic

> Cinematic catastrophes no longer just metaphors, but suddenly quite real

toward visions of terror seemingly plucked out of thin air no longer appears as a contradiction to the reality of modernity, but "it is its 'consistent' further thinking, its application" (Krah 2004, 379; own translation). At the same time, however, apocalyptic films and series not only direct our gaze to the 'end of everything,' but, according to Lillemose, would also point to the possibility of a new beginning:

> *Some disaster films are about saving or re-creating 'our' world, while others are about surviving and coping in an unfamiliar, altered world. Disaster films imagine not only the end of the world, but also the beginning of the one – familiar or alien – that takes its place. And in doing so, they expand our horizons to include the many possible manifestations of 'the end', and point to the many ways of surviving it.* (Lillemose 2021, 47; own translation)

Becoming aware of the impending catastrophe in order to survive it – that could also be the motto for the countless blackout films and TV series that have proliferated in a conspicuous manner in recent years. Films and television series that address catastrophes such as power outages or make them the main topic have always existed – and yet they seem to have anticipated the currently observable greater attention to the topic several years ago. Blackouts are popular as a cinematic stylistic device across genres because they interfere with the familiar normality of modern characters' lives and routines as a disruption, and provoke reactions with

Blackout fictions tell of disruptions of modern life normality as crisis

relatively little narrative and staging effort. The exposition of the blackout films and episodes is usually dominated by images of an all in all carefree and comfortable modern living world with quite banal everyday problems. All the harder, then, is the rift that the blackout tears into this modern idyll: nothing works anymore, everything is suddenly different, and it is unclear how one should behave.

Blackouts are omnipresent in cinematic art forms and at the same time take on different functions in film and television, depending on the dramaturgical and staging intention. They almost always mean a drastic experience for the characters who are suddenly torn out of their modern life reality, which from then on determines the entire way of life and dominates all decision-making situations – even more strongly than we have recently felt with the pandemic (in reality as well as in film and television).

In a growing number of series and feature films, the blackout itself is the actual topic (chapter 3), for example in the series of the same name based on the novel (D 2021). The topic was dealt with in films in Germany and abroad much earlier, for example in *380,000 Volt – Der große Stromausfall* (D 2010) or *The Trigger Effect* (USA 1996). In most of those stories, the blackout remains a temporary exceptional situation and is limited to a specific space within the narrative world: by the end of the film or series, modern normality has been restored by beating back the blackout as an internal enemy of modernization. Thus, the blackout is an ideal

> Blackout thrusts cinematic characters into even greater uncertainty than pandemic

> Chapter 3: Temporary power failure also burdens society and requires creativity

adversary for telling heroine stories, as they appear
in hospital, firefighter and police series with every
new episode. The doctors and nurses of *Grey's
Anatomy* (USA 2005–), for example, have already
been hit by a more or less fatal power outage four
times in the course of their 17-year career – and
have repeatedly been forced to perform emergency
operations in stuck elevators, which requires
courage and creativity. The doctors often work
beyond their limits anyway, for example in *Code
Black* (USA 2015–2017), but the blackout raises the
level of hardness of the everyday heroes' back-
breaking job to a whole new level. Even the
colleagues in the fire department and police are
traditionally regularly affected by blackouts in
television series, whether in *Chicago Fire* (USA
2012), *Station 19* (USA 2018–) or *Brooklyn Nine-
Nine* (USA 2013–) can't do without at least one
obligatory blackout episode. Fire stations are
converted into shelters for freezing citizens, homes
lit by dangerous candlelight have to be evacuated
because of potentially deadly gas leaks, or rescued
with carbon monoxide poisoning from poorly
ventilated, desperately heated rooms. Occasionally,
the initially relentless blackouts inspire creative
solutions, such as when the interim U.S. president
realizes in an episode of *Designated Survivor* (USA
2016–2019) that you don't get a freezing, hungry,
and thus agitated population on your side with the
National Guard, but by pitching in yourself. Some
criminologists develop 'strange methods' when the
blackout hits, so for example in *Bones* (USA 2005–

2017, S06E16), where one dissolves the title-giving bones in pots heated over open fire, loads a cell phone from potatoes and attempts to tap the emergency lighting (what can be dangerous, see fig. 2). And for the journalists in the *Newsroom* (USA 2012–2014), the blackout seems to come just at the right time, because the inevitable break in broadcasting means that creative ideas bubble up that would otherwise be lost in the day-to-day business of lurid stories. When all else fails, the superheroes are on hand with their superhuman powers, whether it's the *Flash* (USA 2015–) or just another of the *New Adventures of Superman (*USA 1993–1997), who has to rescue his Lois from life-threatening situations time and again.

Figure 2: "Mm, what is that smell?" – Removing the bones from the remains is difficult without electricity. The creative forensic scientists from the crime series Bones (S06E16M17) *know how to help themselves, however, and cook the*

evidence by candlelight over assembled Bunsen burners. But when they try to tap the power from the emergency lighting, they almost kill themselves.

Often, it is the entanglement of unfortunate coincidences or uninfluenceable forces of nature that lead to power outages here: violent storms, toppled poles and overloaded substations lead to the shutdown of neighborhoods or entire metropolitan areas. However, there is a striking increase in the number of scenarios in which criminal activities and terrorist actions lead to a blackout. Often, the criminals in blackout films and series act fanatically in the name of an ideology that opposes the electrified modern society (chapter 4). But the oh-so-revolutionary fight against the energy industry can quickly turn into a murder case. Even the terrorists in the Belgian crime series *Unité 42* (2017–) probably did not consider the collateral damage that occurs when they attack the national power grid with hacking commands to transfer billions the moment the banks' digital security systems fail. Meanwhile, they are cool-headedly accepting the risk that the country will be contaminated by chain reactions in equally unprotected nuclear power plants. Less 'noble goals' are pursued by the criminals in the B-movie *Blackout – Terror Just Hit the Lights* (USA 2011), who also target the banks. For such a controlled blackout, you need clever minds that are ready to attack modernity either through the lure of quick big money, as a foreign-determined hostage or lured by a crude ideology. In the same way, however, it is always

Chapter 4: Terrorism and crime as a risk of deliberate provocation of a blackout

such 'nerdy' heroines who help modernity out of the mess in the end. In these moments of greatest need, they show themselves as the saviors of a modern society at war with organized crime and insane would-be revolutionaries.

What these films and series have in common is that the blackout is a problem limited in time and place: as a problem it can be solved, and thus a return to normality remains possible, even if only after severe losses and deprivations. But especially in recent years, such cinematic blackout scenarios have increased, in which a restoration of modernity is in question, perhaps even becomes impossible: a global event, or at least one that encompasses large parts of the world, then disrupts modern society, pushing it beyond the brink of its resilience (chapter 5). The blackout becomes a threshold event that leads from the dearly held modernity to a post-electrified post-modernity: when cell phone networks suddenly stop working, departure boards at train stations and airports indicate every planned trip as "canceled," and cities go dark, these are warning signs that the characters perceive not as an indication of a temporary problem but as an advance notice of a crisis leading to another world. The causes of such an experience of crossing over are manifold in films and television series. In pandemic end-time series such as *Sløborn* (D 2020–) and *The Stand* (USA 2020–2021), civilizations that have lulled themselves into a sense of security no longer manage to recover from an aggressive pathogen and experience the gradual dismantling of

Chapter 5: Blackout signals impending transition to post-modern society modern achievements – both technical and social. In series like *Into the Night* (BE 2020–) and feature films in the style of *Fin* (S 2012), the blame for the impending end of modernity must be placed on astronomical events, preferably a violent solar storm hitting the planet, the radiation caused by a supernova when a star near our solar system reaches the end of its life, or a so-called 'gamma-ray burst' that occurs now and then in the universe for reasons not yet fully understood. Part of the horror of modernity is that humans have learned to create such global catastrophic events themselves as well, whether in the form of an electromagnetic pulse (EMP) caused by nuclear weapons or e-bombs, as it hits the hyperelectrified world of *Radioflash* (USA 2019), or through well-intentioned but unsuccessful experiments, as in the series *Revolution* (USA 2012–2014), which tells of a completely shut-down world after testing a new 'renewable' energy. The blackout is usually also the first harbinger of many an uninvited guest trying to take up residence on Earth, think of the invasion of zombies in films like *World War Z* (USA 2013) or the arrival of extraterrestrial visitors who are not always particularly well-meaning, as in *10 Cloverfield Lane* (USA 2016). Sometimes it is also not entirely clear what exactly has led to the impending doom of the modern age, for example in the Netflix apocalypse film *How It Ends* (USA 2018), where the entire U.S. communications network collapses without notice and rumors of an Armageddon on the West Coast do the rounds; at least no one there can be reached anymore, for whatever reason. As different as these films and series may be, the characters caught up in them seem to have learned early on to read the abrupt onset of blackout as an unmistakable signal that tells them: everything will be different now.

Of course, dealing with this new reality of life usually turns out to be an imposition for the characters, who are accustomed to their comfortable modern coziness – physically, but especially also emotionally (chapter 6). In some psychological 'chamber plays', the impending blackout then appears as a staged-dramaturgical framework for a latent and growing unease of the characters, who seem to be godforsaken and left to their own. The causes of the collapse of modernity does not play any role in the micro- and macrosocial decline that follows the blackout as it becomes a backdrop for the already seething interpersonal conflicts that take root and gradually escalate during the power outage. Typically, in these blackout scenarios, which are often told in a very intimate way and with a small ensemble, people either have to fight for survival in an urban environment that has become hostile, such as in *The Trigger Effect* (USA 1996), or they wait in a constant high-tension atmosphere for their helplessness to escalate, like the anxious hermit figure embodied by Naomi Watts in *The Wolf Hour* (USA 2019), for whom, of all things, the 1977 blackout riots in New York seem like a liberation blow. Even though rural life, traditionally less dependent on electricity, initially seems to offer some protection from the chaos of the powerless

Chapter 6:
Blackout leads to severe psychological stress and social conflict

city, problems are not long in coming there either. In the low-key but intelligent production *Then There Was* (USA 2014), a group of teenagers, after camping in the woods, unsuspectingly returns to a civilization that has been shut down and, denied the luxury of earlier constant availability of all the necessities of life, must fight their way between gangs of brutal free-roaming prison inmates in order to survive. The two sisters of *Into the Forest* (CA 2015), who live with their father in a handsome forest mansion, first learn of the national blackout through the radio and, thanks to their supplies, are initially able to bridge the greatest hardship until social conflicts and dangers gradually invade the small community and threaten to disintegrate it. The Spanish end-time film *Fin* (2012) finds particularly vivid images for the desocializing, isolating power of the blackout: after the power is gone, the members of a group of friends disappear one after the other without a trace – only those who stick together against all odds survive the blackout as the last people in the world.

The blackout in film is not always content to trouble the characters with the immediate consequences of an energy supply failure, such as the collapse of the food supply. As if these very practical consequences were not enough, cinematic blackout scenarios hold in store an arsenal of sinister, occasionally otherworldly, and always quite ominous dangers (chapter 7). For example, the undead and monsters usually announce themselves with a power outage, because in the dark, the fight

Chapter 7:
Horror often waits
in the unexpected
darkness

against them is not only scarier, but also creates quite practical problems, such as the fact that choking hands, stabbing knives and misappropriated chainsaws cannot be seen and fought off so easily in the dark. *The Fog* (USA 1980) does not only make orientation impossible, it also disrupts the power supply – only the radio, thanks to the emergency generator, bravely resists the vengeful sailors. In *Wayward Pines* (USA 2015–2016, S01E10), the hypermobile ravenous mutants cannot be kept in check without an electrified fence. In the pilot of the *Cloverfield* series (USA 2008), the Godzilla-like monster makes itself known at the beginning by a citywide blackout before the military's hopeless battle against the trampling and biting nightmare takes its tiring course. In the horror thrillers *Blackout* (USA 2008) and *Devil* (USA 2010), the otherwise oh-so-harmless elevators become places of horror due to power outages, where sometimes quite secular (murderous), sometimes quite metaphysical (diabolical) madness takes place. And, of course, no zombie fiction can do without blackouts, just think of the never-ending chain of undead series from *The Walking Dead* (USA 2010–2022) and *Black Summer* (USA 2021–) to *All of Us Are Dead* (KR 2022): the fight against the chronically greedy soulless is no child's birthday already under normal conditions, but without electricity it's a real back-breaking job that ties up a lot of your life.

If the dangers associated with the blackout can no longer be controlled in time, the apocalypse looms – and with it the transition to a de-electrified post-modern era. The global power failures provoked by over-committed scientists (*Transcendence,* USA 2014), untypically intense solar activity (*Into the Night*, BE 2020–) and aggressive aliens (*Avanpost*, RU 2020) are regularly so severe in their nature that no modern normality of life can be established. All services and advantages connected with electricity are liquidated – and with it, modernity itself comes to an end (chapter 8). While such a case can hardly be part of real-world crisis prophylaxis, since it naturally takes place beyond modern norms, institutions, and strategies, it is permanently present in films and especially in many recent television series: when in disaster and end-time scenarios such as *Dawn of the Planet of the Apes* (USA 2014), a suddenly chronically sleepless society after the blackout as in *Awake* (USA 2021) or the inevitable zombie apocalypse in the style of *Fear The Walking Dead* (USA 2015 –) everything goes wrong, people find themselves in a *de-modernized*, almost uninhabitable reality. Again and again, the involuntary heroines – the survivors of the global blackout – have to settle into this hostile world, for example in *The Book of Eli* (USA 2010), where thirty years after a devastating world war, all that is left of the Earth is a desert planet, every drop of water leads to murderousness, and you have to pay dearly to charge an MP3 player (in the form of the world's last wet wipes, more valuable than

Chapter 8: Living in a de-electrified post-modernity requires complete conversion of society

gold). Nothing here suggests a failed modernity as much as the absence of electricity. In these post-electrified narrative worlds, nothing is the way it used to be, and yet the memory of a modern life still lives on in the (older) characters – which is what makes coming to terms with the new (dis)order so difficult in the first place. At the same time, the importance of the next generation, for whom modernity is only a myth, is growing: they have decided to settle down in this new world – if necessary, even without electricity. While in the second season of the pandemic series *Sløborn* (D 2020–) the memory of the electrified world of prosperity is still too fresh to let go of the power of the generators and their owners, the people in *Revolution* (USA 2012–2014) have settled into post-modernity as best they can 15 years after a mysterious global blackout. Two decades after a highly lethal pandemic, those who remain in *Station Eleven* (USA 2022) are either living as a nomadic Shakespearean ensemble or have made themselves at home in the airport, where, fortunately, pre-parations were made for their own solar power system shortly before the great catastrophe. For the young generation of *Tribes of Europa* (D 2021–), half a century after the "Black December" of 2029, the old telephones, alarm clocks and battery-operated toys are only useless fossils of long-gone primeval times, while the few still functioning de-vices of the mysterious "Atlantians" are evidence of a far superior intelligence, as if it came from another planet. Only in the contrast of the images of a total shutdown of the modern world, as it appears in these series, the dependence of our very real electrified present becomes clear – and with it also that all prevailing rules, habits and self-evident facts would lose their validity if modernity could not be "switched on" again in time after a blackout.

Almost always, the backdrops of a modernity that has shut down, of otherwise bustling cities that are now dark and cold, provide an aesthetically striking backdrop of the post-modern, of a modern society that has perished from its own successes and now populates its own ruins. In the overall view of films and television series in which blackouts play a role, however, these worst cases fortunately remain the exception. Much more, the blackout creeps in everywhere, regardless of genre and target group, and serves as a popular motif and story driver even in seemingly unsuspicious formats (chapter 9). In sitcoms in particular, a blackout is a popular narrative device: the characters have to cope with the disruption of their everyday normality for a limited period of time before everything returns to 'normal' after 21 or 42 minutes. While in other genres the prolonged blackout pushes societies to the limits of their resilience, in comedy the localized and temporary blackout acts less as a threat and much more as a social catalyst that releases creative energies in the characters and brings them closer together in the end. Sometimes the small blackout also sparks a certain nostalgic longing for a time of less technical progress and (seemingly) "simple" life – and occasionally creates unexpected romantic moments

Chapter 9: Power outages as minimal intervention in the 'perfect world' of comedy enable conflict resolution and thus opportunities for building new communities. Will Ross confess his feelings to his adored Rachel by candlelight in the seventh episode of *Friends* (USA 1994–2004)? In the world of *Desperate Housewives* (USA 2004–2012), will the frozen husband (which Mrs. McCluskey keeps in the freezer to improve her pension) thaw out during the blackout after all and expose the fraud? And can Sheldon from *The Big Bang Theory* (USA 2007–2019) win his best buddy Leonard back to the "Roommate Agreement" once he sees his impressive blackout emergency equipment (including urine-to-drinking-water machine)? In any case, our sitcom friends don't have much to worry about, because unbeknownst to them, they can rest assured that the blackout won't last long. That's also the most important reason why we can laugh at them, because the blackout is only funny if it's over again quickly.

As the brief overview of the seven chapters full of cinematic blackouts should show, cinema and television are literally drawn to the topic. But why have blackout scenarios and themes proliferated in recent years? What blackout narratives do these fictions tend toward – and what does that say about the state of late-modern hyper-connected and highly electrified society? What do the blackout movies and series warn us about, and what does that mean for how we might deal with the threat of widespread blackout in the real world? This book is not meant to scare. Rather, it is intended to show, from the perspective of 'safe entertainment,' the

What do blackout fictions tell us about ourselves? And how can they help us to be better prepared?

diversity of an underestimated problem to which we are not, however, powerlessly at the mercy: with the help of the implicit and explicit recommendations that films and television series convey to us through their speculative scenarios, we can prepare ourselves mentally as well as practically for this situation, which we hope will never occur – so that together we can get through it just fine when the time comes. We can consider ourselves lucky that there are films and series that take on even the most unlikely futures. Since, fortunately, none of us has been affected by a blackout of catastrophic proportions, we can in this way better anticipate the manifold entanglements that would be associated with such an event. The resulting awareness of danger, but also the practical knowledge of how to act, can make a contribution to not being completely surprised if the worst should happen. And last but not least, it may also be a bit of fun to be creeped out and at the same time reassured that these are all ultimately just fairy tales set against a familiar backdrop.

2. ELECTRICITY CRISIS SCENARIOS AND THEIR CAUSES

Hardly anything is more strongly associated with the feeling of modernity than electricity. Living with electrical devices has become so commonplace that we intuitively perceive it, without regular reflection, as modern life par excellence. For Warren (2008, 1), modernity and electricity are synonymous at their core. However, precisely because the use of electricity is something that modern people take for granted and use on a daily basis, most lack basic knowledge regarding the complexities of electricity production, distribution, and, by extension, the potential consequences of a power supply failure (Warren 2018, 20). In the age of an increasingly fragile supply situation, a more active role for individuals as simultaneous consumers and producers of electricity ('prosumers'), and in light of further transformation processes ahead, addressing these issues becomes more urgent for individual private citizens as well. For Heinberg (2009, 166), in view of the already observable and directly impacting climate catastrophe, "humanity's *final* energy problem" (Heinberg 2009, 166) must be solved now: "[W]e cook the planet and ourselves, while losing out on the very economic benefits we are chasing. We have only one narrow timeframe of opportunity for ensuring a desirable future for our species by reducing fossil fuel consumption while developing renewable energy sources and a sustainable economic

Modernity and electricity inextricably linked – but crisis looms if modernization fails

paradigm. The clock is ticking." (Heinberg 2009, 168)

So before we can turn to the power blackout fictions from film and television, we need to get at least a rough overview of the technical, scientific and socio-political discourses on the subject. Unlike other horror scenarios such as rabid zombies and mutant monsters, slimy aliens and aggressive killer robots, part of the appeal of blackout scenarios – much like series and films about pandemics, climate change or cyberterrorism – is fed by the real threat potential, which is dramatized in cinematic entertainment but has a 'kernel of truth'.

A look at the past proves that the blackout is a serious danger that has already materialized several times (although fortunately never in a truly devastating form so far). During a heat wave on the U.S. East Coast, for example, a chain of unfortunate circumstances occurred in New York City on July 13, 1977, as a result of two lightning strikes that struck an ailing power grid, personnel cutbacks, and a heavy load from air conditioning, causing a short circuit and resulting in a serious blackout. While the well-heeled Upper East Side made the best of the situation, spontaneously enjoying dinner on the sidewalks, riots ran rampant, especially in the city's poorer neighborhoods: over the course of the 25-hour blackout, more than 1,000 fires were set, 1,600 stores were looted – and often the looters were even attacked and relieved of their loot, so anarchic were the conditions that night (Pitzke July

Filmic blackouts refer directly and indirectly to 'real' academic discourses

New York City 1977: chain of unfavorable circumstances leads to fatal 25-hour blackout

13, 2007), which also forms the starting point for the film *The Wolf Hour* (cf. chapter 6).

On August 13, 2003, a similar situation led to the largest blackout in North American history, which lasted several days in some regions of the northeastern United States and parts of Canada and affected an estimated 55 million people. Compared to the horror of 1977, there was an overwhelming willingness to help. For example, under the impression of the many failed traffic lights and the traffic chaos, passers-by decided to regulate traffic by hand (Ries et al. 2012, 198), and crimes of opportunity were limited. Nevertheless, the emergency rooms of many hospitals quickly filled with feverish dehydrated patients suffering from heatstroke in the face of air conditioning failure, many of them having been trapped for hours in subway trains and elevators. The incident inspired not least the film *Blackout* (USA 2007), which focuses on the adverse conditions in the poorer neighborhoods of the city.

2003: 55 million affected by power outage on North American East Coast

Since then, one sad blackout record has followed the next. On July 30th, 2012, for example, the blackout with the largest number of people affected to date occurred when hundreds of millions of people (about one-tenth of the world's population) were cut off from the energy supply in India. And just about a year ago, on January 10, 2021, a chain reaction in Pakistan left 210 million people in the dark as a result of a fragile, poorly maintained grid. But the risk of a fatal blackout is not unique to energy-developing countries (like the United States, still suffering from a hopelessly outdated electricity

India, Pakistan, Europe: Blackouts and near-collapses follow each other ever more closely

network). Just days before the incident in Pakistan, a similar situation almost occurred in Europe. On January 8, 2021, a chain of automated protection mechanisms added up to a dangerous imbalance in the European power grid within a minute, which then split into two subgrids and nearly resulted in a Europe-wide blackout. In June 2019, the European power supply was also on the verge of collapse. An investigation showed that speculative short selling on the electricity market had apparently led to an imbalance between supply and demand.

This is precisely the cause of many (near) black-outs, because in order to maintain the European target voltage of 50 hertz, the amount of electricity offered and the amount demanded must be approximately the same – in a continent-wide networked system with several hundred million consumers and an increasing number of producers, this is naturally an error-prone task. The target voltage of 50 oscillations per second is often compared to the human pulse: just like an organism, the 'blood circulation' of the power grid needs a steady rhythm so that the connected devices do not suffer any damage. However, while the human body can briefly rev up to 180 during stress and to less than 60 beats per minute during sleep, the tolerance in the power grid is minimal: here, the alarm bells start ringing at a deviation of 50 millihertz, leaving a tolerance between 49.95 and 50.05 hertz – a narrow corridor that can only be maintained through constant automated and manual interventions, such as emergency shut-

Electricity grids only stable if there is a consistent balance between electricity supply and demand

downs of large industrial consumers. If such emergency measures fail to quickly restore the balance between supply and demand, the grid quickly threatens to collapse (Achermann 2018, 32).

However, severe power outages can also occur as a result of extreme weather events. This happened, for example, on November 25, 2005, in Münsterland, Germany, where unusually heavy snowfall caused power lines to buckle under the weight of the snow, leaving 250,000 people without electricity. Despite the comparatively small number of households affected, damage of about 100 million euros occurred within a few days (Sticher et al. 2010, 35). At the same time, the disaster is often used as an example in the literature to analyze the previously unconsidered problems that can accompany a blackout. For example, some of the emergency generators could not be used immediately due to the lack of uniform standardization of the tank nozzles; frozen products disposed in supermarket parking lots caused a strong odor nuisance and attracted parasites; and people in particular need of help, such as senior citizens, people in need of care and disabled persons, could not be helped directly because it was not clear where these people even lived (Sticher et al. 2010, 35–38).

Extreme weather and natural disasters as frequent causes of local and temporary power outages

The problems encountered, as well as a multitude of other potentially threatening challenges of a blackout, were described by the Office of Technology Assessment at the German Bundestag (TAB) in an extensive commissioned study. The analysis pre-

Bundestag researchers: blackout would be a disaster of national dimensions

sented by the team of researchers led by Thomas Petermann (2010, published in English language
2011) is one of the few comprehensive reports in
the world to highlight the wide range of difficulties
faced by society as a whole as a result of a prolonged
and widespread power blackout in an industrialized
nation. The authors compiled research to describe
the chain of consequences on mass communications,
transportation, food and water supplies, and medical and financial services. Most of the macrosocial
consequences of a blackout presented there can be
intuitively and logically deduced. For example, the
researchers describe a large-scale prolonged blackout as "a combined disaster" of national scope "because the electricity supply reveals interdependencies with other essential infrastructures" (Petermann
et al. 2011, 35), or put another way: in contemporary modern society, virtually all areas of life are dependent on electricity – what only really becomes
apparent when something goes wrong.

This enormous fragility is revealed by the many
examples that the study goes through. For example,
power outages in the U.S. showed that television
stations remained able to broadcast even during a
blackout because they are usually equipped with
generators and emergency studios. However, since
people's homes also lost power, hardly anyone was
able to receive these programs (Petermann et al.
2011, 80). This is dramatic from the point of view
that with a power failure, telephony in private
households is immediately interrupted, the emergency power batteries of phone masts can often only

In the event of a blackout: television continues to broadcast, but no one can receive it; telephone network and Internet fail; radio most important source of information

bridge a power interruption for half an hour, and thus the otherwise constantly available stream of information via telephone and Internet suddenly breaks off. People then sit in a 'black hole' of information shortage, cannot reach their loved ones, and also receive no assured information on how to act. As the examples from film and television also show, the battery-powered radio therefore becomes the most important communicator in such emergencies, as broadcasts can still be received via it when all other mass media have long since ceased to function.

The situation in road traffic would be similarly hopeless. Gates and garage doors would remain locked, tunnels would have to be closed due to the lack of lighting and ventilation, and numerous accidents would occur due to failed traffic lights and lanterns. The resulting mass casualties, in turn, would hit already overstretched fire departments and hospitals, which (although they have emergency generators for a few days of emergency operation) would be overrun by many patients, while medical staff (as well as the many volunteers in disaster control) would in some cases no longer be able to show up for duty because there are no trains and only a few buses. Vehicles can no longer be refueled because gas pumps only work with electricity. The immediate consequences of this medical supply crisis are particularly serious for tens of thousands of kidney patients who have hardly any chance of survival without regular dialysis, just as many people in need

Threat of collapse of transport, medical care and nursing facilities

of care, intensive care patients and residents of institutions for the disabled are dependent on constant care that can hardly be provided under the chaotic conditions of the blackout.

The consequences for society as a whole due to the failure of the drinking water supply appear to be a particular difficulty. Hardly anyone is alerted to the fact that in the event of a power outage, water pumps in buildings as well as waterworks usually stop working and the public water supply thus collapses – dehydration, poor personal hygiene and overflowing toilets are imminent. While authorities can stock emergency wells and activate them in the event of a disaster to at least alleviate the greatest need, sanitary conditions in many buildings (especially on lower floors) force mass evacuations to shelters to prevent epidemics (Karsten 2020, 319–320). Food supplies are also running low quickly, as nowadays neither private households nor supermarkets and wholesalers can afford large reserves – after all, everything seems always available. However, the lack of logistics means that in the event of a blackout, there is a shortage of supplies in stores and wholesalers, while goods requiring refrigeration spoil in households and stores.

Food production is also experiencing a forced pause and horror scenarios at the same time: tens of millions of chickens have to be emergency slaughtered because the barns can no longer be air-conditioned; cows have to be culled by necessity because

Failure of drinking water supply and sewage disposal, lack of supplies in grocery stores

Emergency slaughtering of suffering animals in unheated barns

the animals can no longer be milked and would otherwise die in pain; fodder and grain rot faster because it can no longer be stored correctly.

Many private individuals experience problems after a few days without electricity, as they hardly have any ready-to-eat food (such as canned goods). Since card payments no longer work and hardly anyone still has significant amounts of cash at home, nothing can be bought either, if there is anything left to buy in the stores at all. The German federal government does hold the so-called "Civil Emergency Reserve" (rice, legumes, milk powder, condensed milk) and the "Federal Reserve Cereals" – but these would have to be processed before they could be distributed to the population. The fact that this can hardly be done without electricity has obviously not been taken into account, nor has the problem that gasoline and diesel must first be produced from the "strategic oil reserve" before it can be used to fuel police vehicles, trucks and emergency power generators.

Private households have hardly any supplies – hunger threatens; card payment fails, so hardly any trade possible

The latter is particularly explosive, since nuclear power plants, for example, depend on constant cooling of their fuel elements, which do not cool down directly even after a power failure and shutdown, but continue to produce enormous heat. Generators and fuel must be kept on hand for such purposes. In 2006, for example, such an emergency power supply saved a Swedish nuclear power plant from reactor meltdown and thus saved all of Europe from a Fukushima-like nuclear catastrophe (Welzl

Threat of core meltdowns in nuclear power plants – evacuations not feasible in real

2010, 21). However, since the emergency generators can only bridge a certain period of time, a nuclear super-disaster threatens if the generators cannot be refueled in time. Technical support of damaged nuclear power plants and evacuations of areas affected by impending fallout would not be comprehensively feasible under blackout conditions – with the corresponding health, ecological and economic consequences.

Countless other examples could be cited to show that there is hardly any area of society that would not be directly and severely affected by a blackout. The damage caused by a blackout would be devastating in every respect and is estimated to run into the billions after just one day (Petermann et al. 2011, 65). In this context, the state faces a challenge that can hardly be met by the authorities alone, and not only in Germany. While the fire departments and civil protection are equipped to deal with so-called "spot situations" ("*Punktlagen*") – accidents, fires, release of pollutants – and external help can easily be requested for such regionally limited events; an "area situation" ("*Flächenlage*") such as a supra-regional power blackout quickly creates a situation that systematically overburdens the rescue services and civil protection (Ries et al. 2012, 195). It can therefore realistically be assumed that the state will not be able to compensate for all the services lost in the event of an incident.

Disaster management not prepared for nationwide or pan-European wide-area situation

Of course, there are a large number of legal requirements and government precautionary actions to keep damage to a minimum, for example in the form of contracts for the preferential supply of fuel to public authorities and hospitals (Ries et al. 2012, 202). The *"TankNotStrom"* ("Refueling Emergency Power") research project, which has since expired, also aimed to improve the supply of fuel to critical infrastructures. Considerations have gone so far that German fire departments are experimenting with whether they would be able to set up makeshift refueling stations with their usual response equipment – in some cases with success (Mayer et al. 2017, 79). In Vienna, a so-called "barrier cable network" ("Sperrkabelnetz") was set up to protect important facilities such as hospitals from automatic load shedding (Welzl 2010, 21). TAB experts have also made proposals, for example, to provide nationwide "one [retail trade] branch outlet suitable for coping with disasters for every 10,000 inhabitants and also specifying the provision, in every federal state, of a food warehouse that is equipped with an extensive storage facility, means of communication and emergency power generator" (Petermann et al. 2011, 211) – but this has been implemented just as little as the recommended construction of self-sufficient and thus less failure-prone "isolated network solutions [*"Eigenstrominsellösungen"*] based on renewable energies" (Petermann et al. 2011, 230).

Creative ideas on how the state can still act in the event of a blackout – but hardly ever implemented

There seem to be enough technical ideas and intelligent solutions. However, the prevailing opinion among experts is that there is hardly any significant awareness of the risk of a blackout in politics, the economy and the civilian population, and that there are at most only theoretical approaches to networking among social actors (Ries et al. 2012, 203). Although the Corona pandemic and the war in Ukraine have brought some attention to the problem of supply gaps, this has hardly translated into a greater willingness to engage in expedient disaster preparedness among the civilian population and the business community. At the same time, the potential damage that could occur has continued to grow in recent years due to the ever-increasing level of technological interconnectedness. TAB experts are therefore not the only ones to come to the alarming conclusion that Germany, including its population, would be literally overrun by the "cascading damage effects" of the "combined disaster" ["*Verbundkatastrophe*"] blackout (Petermann et al. 2011, 233). Since it would hardly be possible for the state to take complete precautions for such a national crisis, even with unlimited resources, individual disaster preparedness is of particular importance in modern civil defense: Without a "resilient" population, i.e., one that is practiced in self-help and thus able to withstand it, a society is at the mercy of a widespread and long-lasting crisis scenario such as a blackout.

Awareness of blackout increases, but little significant preparation by government, business, households

The list of possible causes for a blackout is long: human or technical errors in power plants or control centers, market speculation, criminal machinations, terrorist actions, armed conflicts, computer sabotage (cyberattacks), high sickness rates due to pandemics, and extreme weather events provide the perfect breeding ground for crises in energy supply (Schneider 2018, 159–161; cf. chapter 3). In contrast, the current scientific as well as political debate focuses on the opportunities and challenges that arise with the modernization of electricity production and infrastructure toward renewables. To understand the potential problems, it is worth taking a look at the past. Before the start of the energy transition, relatively few and therefore very powerful power plants supplied a relatively continuous and therefore base-loadable amount of electricity. Since this stable and easily switched-on-and-off electricity was mainly generated from fossil fuels and fissile material, this 'comfortable' production method came at the price of devastating environmental and climate damage. Not only because of the interference with nature, but also because of the impending shortage of fossil fuels alone, a switch to renewable energies is inevitable. With its Electricity Feed-in Act of 1991 and the successor regulation of the Renewable Energy Sources Act of 2000, Germany was particularly progressive in this respect in international comparison: now not only could every individual become an electricity producer, since electricity from renewable energies – for example from

Multiple causes, especially in view of overdue modernization of electricity production

the solar cell on the roof – was preferentially fed into the grid and compensated separately.

This desirable development is associated with some technical and economic challenges which, from today's perspective, have obviously been neglected or have not enough been foreseen. On the one hand, renewable energies 'naturally' generate electricity only when the wind moves the rotor blades of the turbines and solar rays shine on the photovoltaic systems. In Switzerland, in vivid contrast to the steady electricity from conventional combustion and nuclear power plants ("*Bandstrom*"), wind and solar are referred to as 'flutter electricity' ("*Flatterstrom*"): how much electricity is produced at any given moment simply depends on the weather and varies greatly throughout the day, sometimes from one moment to the next (Achermann 2018, 54). In addition, the regions with a favorable location in terms of new energy (for example, the windy north of Germany) are not always the strongest consumers (such as the industrially strong south of Germany), so electricity must first be transported to where it is needed (Karsten 2020, 315). At the same time, the 'just in time' electricity generated from renewables cannot be easily stored and must be consumed at the moment of its production. However, in order to maintain the delicate balance in the power grid and thus the target voltage of 50 Hertz, production and consumption must be in harmony.

Energy transition brings with it irregularly flowing electricity that has to be transported a long way

Obviously, these core problems could be over-come by creating electricity storage facilities, plan-ning for excess capacity and massively expanding the grid. However, the current situation deviates from the ideal, worldwide and also in Germany. With a demand of about 80 gigawatts of electricity production, the renewable energies available in Ger-many are often not even able to supply 10 gigawatts, and on days with little wind and sun, the feed-in even falls below one gigawatt (Paulitz and Klöckner 2021). If the perspective is indeed to be an almost complete switch to renewables, a "virtually 100 per-cent backup system" for wind and solar energy is realistically needed to cushion lulls (Achermann 2018, 52; own translation). This is possible, but also expensive, as losses are incurred in converting 'sur-plus' electricity into storable forms (Borner and Schips 2018, 23). So more security of supply is also reflected in the price of electricity. At the same time, these technologies themselves are not always exactly environmentally friendly, considering the necessary landscape interventions for pumped-storage power plants and the ecological burdens caused by recy-cling batteries.

Expansion of renewables remains sluggish, lack of storage and backups

While Germany with its access to the sea and favorable locations for wind and solar power plants could easily solve these problems, other countries, such as Switzerland, will remain permanently de-pendent on imports of electricity and thus on an ef-ficient European power grid (Achermann 2018, 73). But even here, the problems have so far been sat out mainly by 'importing' conventionally produced

Many energy producers make it difficult to restart power grid after a blackout

electricity from abroad to Germany (Karsten 2020, 315). According to Achermann (2018, 55–56; own translation), the decentralized organization of energy feed-in that has emerged in the meantime also creates "new problems in the distribution grids (e.g. due to voltage problems, grid reinforcements that become necessary, harmonic waves, difficulties in restarting after major grid interruptions, communication with prosumers, data protection, etc.)". In the event of a blackout, 'reconnecting' the grid today would be much more complicated than in the past, as the myriad production units would first have to be reconciled or 'synchronized' (Borner and Schips 2018, 29). Whether this works so easily under real conditions is something that (fortunately) no one has ever had to try out. Thus, for Karsten (2020, 318), the increasingly decentralized structure of the power grid leads "on the one hand to a rise in resilience against massive, punctual impacts (power plant fires, terrorist attacks, etc.), but on the other hand to a reduction in resilience due to a greater need for control and thus against low-threshold impacts such as cyber-attacks" (Karsten 2020, 318; own translation).

Blaming the energy transition as such for this misery is a cheap excuse. If, for example, the renewables that are used particularly intensively in our latitudes, wind and sun, are not always equally available, this does not mean that we have to fatalistically surrender to this fact. We can build more pumped-storage power plants in areas suitable for this purpose, which store energy surpluses by pumping up

Not the necessary energy turnaround, but half-hearted implementation increases risk of blackout

water and simply release it again when needed (this not only helps the climate, but also in the event of an energy bottleneck, by the way also after a possible blackout). One can push ahead with grid expansion in order to pipe offshore electricity to the energy-intensive south or to the Scandinavian countries, which are ideal for pumped-storage power plants. With 'power to gas' and 'power to liquid', the previously non-material electricity from renewables could be 'cast into shape' again and burned with conventional engines. Other innovative forms of power generation and management could be used, from tidal power plants to incorporating the storage capabilities of electric cars to interconnecting decentralized power generation units into a larger 'virtual power plant' as demonstrated in studies by the German technical universities TU Berlin and BTU Cottbus.

The fact that the energy turnaround is necessary seems inevitable in view of scarce fossil fuels, and not only for climate protection reasons. The factors currently under discussion that could promote a blackout during the transformation phase from conventional to contemporary energy production are comparatively easy to eliminate – all that is needed is political will and, above all, the commitment to invest in future technologies instead of yesterday's solutions. Even if ultra-conservative and right-wing populist self-made 'experts' would wish otherwise: in times of scarce gas reserves, exploding oil prices, dependence on raw material imports

Fear of blackout is abused for economic and political interests

from fragile states and ever new safety gaps in nuclear power plants, it seems, diplomatically formulated, to be driven by extraneous purposes and is
hardly logically justifiable to misuse the necessary
and (according to common sense) logical process of
modernizing the energy industry as a scapegoat for
a supply threat. In the film *The Coming Days* (D
2010), for example, it is precisely these problems –
which appear to be quite present – that arise from
mutual dependencies and a geopolitically unclear
situation, leading to a war on resources, impoverishment and terrorism (cf. fig. 3). Whoever rages
against the modernization of energy supply under
the pretext of a blackout allegedly threatened by it,
in order to make political chapter out of it, must allow himself to be reproached in the case of the catastrophe for having made his contribution to the
failure of modernity.

Critically questioning whether the process of
change in the energy industry and policy has succeeded at all times, whether all individuals have
made their appropriate contribution, and where
(quick) lessons need to be learned from past mistakes is an ongoing and important task that affects
us all. This book can therefore also be understood
as an offer to consider the consequences that
threaten us if the timely modernization of electricity
production and distribution does not succeed.
There is still time to avert the worst – but if the
worst-case scenario should actually occur, it will
hardly be possible to neutralize the consequences by
appropriate means. The Corona pandemic proves

Pandemic shows:
elimination of
damage always
more expensive
than prophylaxis –
intervention
needed now

that inadequate precautions in the event of an incident will have to be operated at great expense afterwards, resulting in a lack of liquidity for other important social projects – not least for the energy
revolution itself. Against the backdrop of blackout
scenarios from movies and television, we can only
hope that we do not deprive ourselves of the room
for maneuver for important changes by once again
belatedly taking precautions and expensively iron-
ing out earlier mistakes. Otherwise, there is the
threat of an endless loop of expensive crises, with
the costs of fighting their causes eventually becoming unaffordable. We are still (just) 'ahead of the
game' – but for how much longer?

*Figure 3: "It looks like the war won't be worth it much longer" – The German
feature film* Die kommenden Tage *(102) shows the Federal Republic of Germany scarred by the struggle for oil, in which the only way out of the crisis is
to set up solar power plants wherever possible, even in the middle of the city if
necessary. The main character writes to her brother in a letter to the front: "I
love it. Because it gives me hope that you'll be back soon." (own translations)*

This brief outline should show that numerous scientific papers describe theoretically probable or plausible consequences of a widespread blackout, often against the backdrop of shorter, spatially limited power outages and technical impact assessments. As important as the work of research specialists is, their sophisticated articles often remain abstract, unapproachable, and thus not relatable or comprehensible to an audience outside the field. Researchers and experts also warned of a dangerous pandemic long before the outbreak of the Corona virus – without any significant consequences (such as the recommended stockpiling of protective equipment). Movies and TV series, on the other hand, do not care about scientific principles, accuracy, verifiability, or methodological carefulness, but they can still be understood as a specific form of knowledge order that, however, obeys different rules than an academic text.

Filmic art forms not only show in an impressive way that societies that do not address these challenges seriously and in time have to struggle with problems that threaten their existence and, in the worst case, end up in a post-electrified age, for example like in the German Netflix series *Tribes of Europa* (D 2021–). They also make – consciously and unconsciously, sometimes overtly and sometimes in code – imaginative offers to prevent, avert and overcome crises, often going far beyond the tangible management options that can be found in studies and official recommendations on the subject.

Science abstract – film and television plastic

Film and television show consequences of a blackout – and possible remedies

Those who have picked up this book expecting to find in it a step-by-step matching of academic discourses on blackout with those that develop film and television may be disappointed. The fact that certain parallels between fiction and academic debate are inevitable is due to the very fact that screenwriters deal with the state of knowledge in the field, with probable courses of events from the perspective of the sciences. This makes it possible to avoid obvious errors and improbable plot developments, which would also make a fictional narrative implausible and thus no longer invite empathy.

Filmic art forms refer to professional discourses, but deal with them in a playful way

In this book, however, it is much more a matter of allowing film and television to speak for itself largely free of external constraints, and to formulate precisely what is not written in academic treatises: How do the characters behave in this fictitious extreme situation when confidence in the state's crisis management of their reality decreases? What happens if a blackout lasts longer than two weeks and hope of a quick return to normal modern conditions fades? And above all: How do the heroines of these scenarios know how to help themselves, and can we 'learn' something from them for our own lives?

Film and television can speculate freely and thus deal with previously unexamined questions

Most papers, including the most important and comprehensive TAB study, do not make any statements on these questions, because it would tip over into the speculative – there is simply a lack of knowledge methods, since it is in the nature of things that a widespread, long-lasting power blackout can hardly be experimentally simulated and a

What we know about the blackout, we know only from movies and television

field study would also only be possible in a replication, but there is – fortunately – no experience with such a scenario so far. No sure statements can be made about the psychological consequences on the individual as well as about probable socio-psychological effects – even if theoretical texts hardly miss the opportunity to emphasize that one should not expect the mass panic, hysteria and looting rage 'known from film and television'. Much more interesting, however, seem to be precisely those questions about which, for exactly those epistemological reasons, one has not yet been able to think comprehensively in research, but which are raised and dealt with by the fictional play with futures.

This book is therefore primarily concerned with those problems that film and television 'exclusively' address and play out: with the fears and hopes that emerge in such works, with the significance of seemingly aberrant courses of action for the self-image of modern society, and with the potential for creative ideas for scopes of action and methods of coping. Why do we tell each other, via blackout films and series, of all things, these stories – at first glance plucked out of thin air – of a world in which the power has not only gone out, but has never returned? What does the sudden darkness in film and television stand for? What does it point to as metaphor or allegory? And what does this ultimately mean for modern society, in which precisely those films and series circulate in a conspicuously lively manner?

What do blackout fictions tell us about our society, our fears and hopes, our future?

3. THEY GROPE IN THE DARK: POWER FAILURES AND THEIR HEROINES

The long list of films and television series that are either exclusively dedicated to blackouts or where power outages at least play a role proves the undeniable presence of the topic in cinematic popular culture. But not all blackouts are the same. Just as in reality where we have often smaller, regional and temporary *power failures* and only very rarely widespread and long-lasting *blackouts*, different types of blackout scenarios can also be distinguished in feature films and series. Localized and temporary blackouts have their home in single episodes of series of all kinds, especially in hospital and firefighting series as well as in crime and action hero narratives. Occasionally, there are also feature films (mostly television films) that devote a full-length narrative to the topic. On the other hand, there are films and series in which the blackout affects entire countries or even the entire world, and where it is uncertain, whether the problem can be solved in the course of the movie night or the series season. The causes can be realistic or fantastic, but the consequences are always very concrete, regularly devastating and hardly manageable. Sometimes the modern world doesn't get its act together – a world without electricity becomes 'the new normal'. This is when a post-modernity sets in, and all that remains are optionally nostalgic, mythical or hated memories of the former electrified modern

Power failures are limited in time and space; blackout is area-wide and long-lasting

times. These often post-apocalyptic series and films then focus on the coping strategies of a life without electricity in an unwound modernity.

This chapter, however, will initially deal with the first of these three categories: here, the blackout disrupts the normality of the familiar series reality or the modern carefreeness shown in the film exposition – but it is clear from the outset that it is a localized and temporal disruption and that the return to everyday routines is only a matter of time. Because the surrounding is not equally affected by the power outage area, in these film and series realities other cities and states, hospitals and departments, external experts and, if necessary, superhuman rescuers can quickly rush to the rescue and prevent greater damage (unlike the blackout, hitting whole countries). Until then, however, the film and television characters have to face the major and minor challenges of this situation. While the population can simply 'sit out' the blackout at home (if they have prepared themselves accordingly), during which most stores, offices and schools will have to remain closed anyway, the catastrophe primarily affects those who work in the areas where the damage is to be managed: the energy suppliers as well as the fire departments, police and disaster control. Relevant blackout films and series focus their narratives on these everyday heroes who are otherwise not the center of attention.

Power outage fictions tell stories from the perspective of otherwise invisible everyday heroines

This is also the case in the (not exactly critically acclaimed) German TV film *380.000 Volt – Der Große Stromausfall* ("The Great Blackout") from 2010. Due to an initially inexplicable failure in a transformer station and the subsequent line overload, it suddenly goes dark in otherwise brightly lit Berlin – only the headlights of cars still illuminate the streets. Under the (perhaps a bit too quickly) escalating conditions in the film, the city's many 'angels' must demonstrate improvisational talent. Hospitals do have emergency generators, but they also have to work in an emergency, which they do here (and in blackout fictions in general) only to a limited extent. Thus, surgeons operate in the light of flashlights without the usual technical support, while technicians assemble an emergency solution from laptop batteries in order to get the most important devices up and running again. At the same time, the intensive care units are full of accident casualties and gunshot victims. In the rest of the city, police are fighting rioters, but are visibly overwhelmed. Some particularly 'order-loving' citizens hijack police vehicles to carry out vigilante justice. The fire department, on the other hand, is overwhelmed with calls for help, because fires keep breaking out in buildings as people try to warm themselves with open fires or light candles. In general, it is difficult for the population and the authorities to maintain an overview, because cell phones and most landline telephones fail. Thus, radio becomes the most important source of information. Some allotment gardeners still have a

Hospitals and police quickly reach their limits, communication only possible via radio and walkie-talkies

small television set with battery power, and car drivers are kept up to date thanks to the radio. The employees of the energy provider itself, on the other hand, would be completely lost if they didn't have their handheld radios (walkie talkies) – at least they thought of a backup here.

Under these chaotic conditions, shift supervisor Radtke must determine the real cause of the problem in the power company's clueless control center before the city becomes ungovernable. But instead of a technical defect, she encounters a hand-wringing intrigue: board members of the power company had blatantly staged the blackout to force the construction of a new power plant and rail against the 'environmental lobby'. In the midst of the corrupt conspiracy, the clever engineer sees only one ally: the somewhat unruly but dedicated technician Volanski, who joins her in uncovering the intrigues. Armed with a screwdriver and a candy bar, he not only repairs the sabotaged transformer, but also collects evidence to settle the score with the criminal board of directors: it is obvious that the network has been poorly maintained and broken over the years, that too few staff have been hired for too much work, and that such a power network is "not a chain of department stores!" (own translation) Finally, the blackout is not only the occasion for an overdue debate about the modernization of the city grid: with Radtke and Volanski, two hard-working idealists have become a couple in the fight against the blackout.

Technical staff must compensate for consequences of savings in materials and personnel in the power grid

While the scenario of *380.000 Volt* is fictional (and unfortunately riddled with some technical and logical errors), the U.S. television film *14 Hours* (2005) is based on true events as they took place in 2001 during Hurricane Allison in the Houston area. Told from the perspective of the local medical and nursing staff, the film is somewhat clichéd in its character constellation and dialogue, but at least quite realistic from a technical point of view, and tells the story of the grueling 14 hours in the city's Memorial Hermann Hospital during a power outage. While surgeries are being performed, premature babies are being cared for and intensive care patients are being kept alive in the hospital as usual, the hurricane brings with it vast amounts of precipitation that floods into the hospital's basement. The blood units and transplant organs also stored in the basement are hurriedly brought to safety, but the nurses put themselves in danger. When the power supply collapses citywide, the emergency generators required by law are initially able to maintain the most important functions so that operations that have begun can be completed. However, the protective walls around the generators are far too low and not designed for complete flooding of the basement – the only option left is an emergency shutdown to prevent worse.

As the hospital lies in darkness and the water gradually rises to the first floor, it becomes apparent that the pumps kept on hand for such cases will not be able to push the water back fast enough. In the meantime, a double burden typical of hospitals

Emergency generators in hospitals can temporarily alleviate greatest need – but prone to failure

Hospital staff experience double burden: treating more patients under more difficult conditions

becomes apparent during a power blackout: on the one hand, the lack of equipment and the darkness make the work much more difficult and, in some cases, it cannot be done satisfactorily at all; on the other hand, more and more patients arrive who are affected by the consequences of the power blackout (through accidents, hypothermia, exhaustion). At the same time, the helpers are burdened with the emotional responsibility to "do their best" and to help all patients equally well, even if material and personnel are limited.

The staff tries to improvise as best they can in this situation. Fortunately, the "old school" nurses still know how to help themselves without modern equipment: they check oxygen saturation, for example, by looking at the discoloration of the skin, they measure blood pressure and pulse manually, and oxygen is administered by hand using a resuscitation bag. The nurses are proud of their ability to keep the patients alive without the help of machines, but of course the failure of the automatic care system requires much more energy than is available. Although the employees work to exhaustion, there is no alternative to evacuation when the oxygen runs out.

Certain medical devices can be temporarily replaced manually – but that is costly and inefficient

In the film, the disaster control authority is completely overwhelmed with the task of transferring the many patients to surrounding hospitals, and there is obviously hardly any cooperation with other state and federal authorities. It quickly becomes clear that without the many volunteers who spontaneously turn up to work in the face of the

Disaster management overwhelmed with relocation of patients – many volunteers, emergency rations and prioritization criteria are needed

need seen in the media, the coming challenges could not be met: bedridden people have to be prepared for transport, and burn victims have to be safely packed before they can be carried down the stairwell over several floors with as little vibration as possible. It would certainly be helpful if the workers did not have to make PB&Js in the hallway; an emergency supply of ready-to-eat meals would be the more practical solution. In the meantime, the nurses and doctors have to prioritize the patients according to their need and ability to be transported – a task that can hardly be solved satisfactorily with 300 patients.

Particularly touching in the film are the images of helpless premature babies, who are only kept alive by the marvels of modern medicine: they need a continuous supply of moist warm air and oxygen (brought about by the incubator), sometimes also infusions, supplemental oxygen or ventilation; sensitive devices monitor the vital functions of the too-small baby. Because all these devices have only batteries for short bridges (until the emergency generators kick in), all these functions have to be taken over by hand in the worst case. A similar situation arises in the hospital series *Grey's Anatomy* in the episode "Perfect Storm" (S09E24), when likewise the aggregates do not start (here it is air in the fuel line) and, as the parents complain, nobody has thought of spare batteries. However, these would only postpone the problem. The senior neurosurgeon at the "Grey+Sloan Memorial Hospital", Derek Shepherd, therefore suggests in an

Premature infants particularly affected, but can be ventilated by hand if necessary

obvious way that the parents, who are present anyway (and so far mainly disturbing, as they are justifiably concerned), could take over the manual ventilation of their children. They initially react skeptically, rejecting or fearful – but are then persuaded, since it is not only urgently necessary, but also easily manageable: actually, one only has to rhythmically squeeze the ventilation bag (cf. fig. 4). As long as the task is manageable and an end to the blackout is foreseeable, such an emergency situation can even lead to new community experiences, because the parents obviously feel a moment of special bond with their children, whose helplessness will probably never again be as evident as in this situation. Of course, this is not a permanent state of affairs, especially since the premature babies cannot be moved by conventional means – the tiny creatures are too delicate, even fragile, for a trip in an ambulance. Only when the National Guard finally arrives after *14 Hours,* the small humans can be safely transported to surrounding hospitals by helicopter.

Since the danger of power failure in these films and series seems, all things considered, manageable and temporary, such scenarios are characterized by pragmatic characters who, hero-like, attempt to alleviate the greatest need through individual sacrifice. This requires not only courage and perseverance, but also a wealth of ideas and a willingness to take unconventional measures. The latter, in particular, are what make the blackout narratives so appealing, since they mean that rules and taboos can

Standard care and provision for emergencies are in budgetary competition with each other

or even must be broken every now and then. In the *Grey's Anatomy* episode "Bring the Pain" (S02E05), for example, the head of surgery is angry that the defective generator, which had already caused problems during the last blackout, was not replaced – although he himself had decided that a new MRI machine should rather be purchased for the money. Because savings were made on preventive care in favor of chronically underfunded standard treatment, the next power outage will have a number of curious consequences here.

Figure 4: When the power fails in hospitals, the premature babies are particularly hard hit. In Grey's Anatomy (S09E24M35), parents have to take responsibility themselves and develop an unexpected special closeness to their offspring in the moment of need. But how long can manual breathing assistance via resuscitator be sustained?

Since the problem is limited to the hospital, that is in the 2nd season even still quite cheerful (whereby the series becomes altogether from year to year ever more dark). In this episode, one patient suffers under the Blackout in a special way. Because of chronic severe back pain due to a herniated disc, his vertebral bodies are to be joined. Since he reacts hypersensitive to all usual pain medicines, his treating physician – regularly scrolling through professional journals – had prescribed to him to reduce the pain by the consumption of porno films up to the relief-providing procedure, which obviously took effect. The doctors and especially female doctors are initially skeptical, but let Dr. Shepherd convince them of the clear data, because the films would release painkilling endorphins. But when the power goes out, so does the TV, and the suffering becomes unbearable for the poor patient. So the attending physician, Dr. Christina Yang, has to come up with something to help the patient, who is whimpering in pain. She finally sits down on the neighboring bed and tells – at first somewhat reservedly, finally with a certain routine hard on the edge of enjoyment – a (probably fictitious) story of three nurses soaping each other up in the shower ("Marta was the naughtiest nurse of all, because she knew how to...", M32). The fantasies distracting from the pain actually calm the man down, but fortunately the power comes back on just in time – and with it the tape recorder.

Emergency surgery in an elevator, unconventional pain therapies: emergency situation requires willingness to use creative methods

The main heroine, Dr. Meredith Grey, is less fortunate. In season 9, she has to give birth to her child with serious complications – during the blackout. But that's not all: because the inexperienced doctors are overwhelmed by the situation, Meredith – while she herself is already undergoing surgery in the lower abdomen! – has to give her pupils precise instructions on what they have to observe during the complicated Caesarean section (but she has already survived worse, including a plane crash and a rampage). Meanwhile, the janitor lies unconscious in the basement, having been electrocuted by all the water between the electrical equipment while trying to get the generators running again. His boss, who then tries to turn the power back on for him, also gets a shock, sustains burns and faints. It is not until the following episode that the colleagues find him and finally figure out that the flooded room is under voltage. Meanwhile, the devastated hospital has filled up with many people in need of help, which in turn quickly leads to a shortage of material. When the key to a medicine cabinet can't be found in all the tumult, the resolute Dr. Bailey unceremoniously smashes the cabinet with an IV stand – and at the same time unloads some of her rage, which stems from the feeling of (in itself avoidable) powerlessness during the blackout. In the midst of all the confusion, one wishes the shift supervisors had a megaphone – and, above all, that their generators would eventually kick in.

Power outage necessitates constant improvisation to staff's breaking point – frustration when power outage is avoidable

The inevitable elevator scene counts to the classics of all blackout episodes, especially in a hospital series (see fig. 5). In *Grey's* two-part power failure spectacle "Blowin' in the Wind" (S15E08), the generators finally work for once, but their output is not enough to run the power-intensive elevators. So beyond the elevators, operations continue frantically as usual, but patients are no longer getting to their treatments and surgeries. Those trapped in the elevators are resorting to bizarre methods of necessity. Due to the storm that led to the power outage, patients have been admitted with 'atypical' accidental injuries, includeing a gentleman with a flying license plate stuck in his chest that appears to have affected his heart. The doomed patient has to be operated on in the stuck elevator, i.e. 'opened up' – and is lucky that he is locked up with Owen and Teddy, who have experienced crueler things as medical officers at war. In peacetime, of course, the doctors properly use a hammer and Lebsche sternum chisel to smash the sternum – but here, the heavy battery of the ECG machine and, of all things, the fateful license plate itself (bent to shape on the hygienically dubious grab handle) have to serve as surgical instruments. Meanwhile, the colleagues massage the bag of blood and the open heart with their hands.

Doctors are forced to use risky methods, because without care fatal consequences are imminent

All these rather brutal methods (which are justifiable here only because of the otherwise certain death of the patient) could be safely dispensed with if the emergency generators would finally do what they were purchased for. It would also be helpful if the fire department would prioritize requests from hospitals rather than first freeing the less vulnerable shoppers from supermarket lifts. Because neither happens, the elevator doors have to be opened again with brute force – which costs a technician his legs because the elevator starts moving again at the very moment of the rescue operation.

Forcible opening of elevators must be prioritized and carried out with extreme caution – risk of amputation

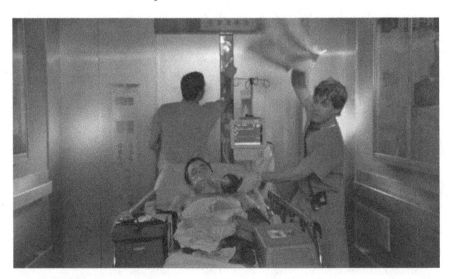

Figure 5: Emergency surgery in a stuck elevator is one of the standard situations of power failure episodes in hospital series, as here in the episode "Bring the Pain" of Grey's Anatomy (S02E05M22). The transfer of material through the thin door slot is a dangerous thing between floors, should the power return at the wrong moment (as in the episode "Shelter from the Storm", S15E09M24) – then amputations are imminent.

Ingenuity combined with a cool head is also needed in the event of a power blackout beyond the power utilities and hospitals, especially in the fire departments and the police just as much as in the government. For example, in the episode "In the Dark" (S02E14), the *Designated Survivor* (USA 2016–2019), who is the only administration official to survive an attack and become the U.S. president from one day to the next, has to fight a city-wide power outage in the federal capital of Washington, D.C. He is the only one to survive the attack in the political series. While he is sitting in the White House overlooking the city having dinner (in a hurry, as usual), he has to watch as one block after another goes dark. The competent, assertive and at the same time almost superhumanly sympathetic head of state lets out only a "Son of a bitch!" (translated more statesmanlike in the German dubbed version as: "That's impossible!", M09; own translation). In the obligatory briefing in the subterranean 'Situation Room', the president learns not only that this is a hacker attack intended to weaken confidence in government institutions, but also that some creditors of the bankrupt U.S. are suddenly tired of waiting for their installments under these conditions. It is therefore advisable to turn the power back on as soon as possible in order to avert several simultaneously looming sovereign crises.

Hackers want to undermine trust in state institutions with attack on power supply

In the midst of the ghost town, the White House remains the only fully functioning government facility – at least for eight hours, as long as the generators still have enough fuel before rationing begins. Here, too, handheld radios replace the otherwise omnipresent Blackberrys which now are only useful as expensive flashlights. The city's dedicated and popular mayor asks the president to set up her crisis center here, because the city hall is also without power – and the city administration is thus *powerless*. In the city, which is plagued by high unemployment, severe gentrification and public underfunding, emotions quickly run high, as the city leader explains: "Our tax base barely covers our essential services. When the government doesn't fulfill its duty to keep the lights on, all that frustration boils over." S02E14M22) Despite all the mutual sympathy, a dispute arises between the municipality and the federal government: Should the National Guard be used to crack down on looters and rioters and enforce the state's monopoly on the use of force by any means necessary – or would it be better to let the local security forces do their job in order to prevent further alienation of the population from the state? The mayor, who herself lives in the Bellevue neighborhood (not exactly known as Washington's nightlife district), wants to prevent the latter at all costs: if martial law were imposed, her community would not recover.

Disproportionate harshness of law enforcement can lead to alienation of the population from the government

Figure 6: In the inevitable blackout episode of Designated Survivor *(S02E14M33), the superhumanly sympathetic U.S. president isn't above handing out bottles, baby food and blankets at an emergency shelter with the mayor. The nervous population visibly appreciates the fact that the people's representatives are not hiding in their generator-secured seat of government.*

Impressed by their civic-mindedness, the president makes a last-minute plea to remind the population that this is their community they're breaking, and plans "some old-fashioned retail politics" (33): instead of bringing in heavy guns, the president goes shoulder-to-shoulder with the mayor – under the watchful eye of the bodyguard, of course – into the thick of the action, they distribute emergency rations in the community centers, thank the firefighters and address some pathetic but thoughtful words to the visibly impressed people (see fig. 6): "We all need to work together to make our home better. And this is our home. [...] So we'll

Presence of political staff during blackout critical to motivate population to participate

make you a deal. We'll roll up our sleeves if you will." (M34) While the skeptical security advisor doesn't really want to believe that such a thing works, the charming press spokesman, of course, knows about the power of words, and on closer inspection, a few really sincere sentences are sometimes more effective than an expensive intervention. The president is also impressed – and has the mayor, who has been baptized with fire, elected vice president.

In general, the hardship of the power blackout tempts the film and television characters time and again to also personally outgrow themselves and to question their previous routines and attitudes. The idealistic journalists of *The Newsroom* (USA 2012–2014) initially set out to leave behind the sensationalism of commercialized television news and return to the roots of investigative research, but quickly find themselves up against quota pressure. Because they feel compelled, in favor of higher market shares, to report on bogus news circulated in the lurid tabloid press and have to throw important political topics out of the program to do so, the team's morale is on the floor. With the self-absorbed publicity-hungry interview guest already in the studio, the producer (struggling with professional ethics and self-respect) asks for a divine sign – and, just in time for the halfway point of the double episode, is seemingly answered: the recording of the hated "Tragedy Porn" (S01E08/09) is cancelled, because a few too many air conditioners must have been turned on that hot day, and (once again) the

Broadcasting needs fail-safe systems to remain broadcast-capable in any situation

backup generator won't kick in ("What about all the redundancies?" – "There's a round of budget cuts before you got and they cut some of the redundancies because..." – "Don't say it!" – "... they thought they were redundant." S02E09M03). In an emergency situation, the public is particularly dependent on reliable information to prevent rumors and conspiracy theories from spreading – backup power supply cost-cutting turns out to be a very bad idea.

Instead of regretting the situation, the head of recording – inspired by her 'spiritual' experience – begins to rave about a new journalistic beginning: she says, they will simply record the program in the open air and, through the difficult task, finally "we become a team again" (M04). All that is needed is a table, a few cameras, mics, lights, an outside broadcast van, of course a few power generators (they still have to be bought, good luck!), police protection – and above all: the desire for an adventure, which is visibly written all over the faces of the excited newsmakers. "I say, the power going out is the best thing that ever happened to us!" (M06), the heartthrob journalist shouts ecstatically into the excited office – when at that very moment the lights come back on, and work continues as usual. Maybe it was just a few minutes of unfounded reverie about a different way of working, maybe even about a different way of *living*, but even if nothing comes of the plans for the emergency show that welds them together, a rethink begins: If we're going to report on tabloid topics, why not do it with ambition and exclusive guests? And shouldn't we cancel a long-

Power blackout as a common challenge opens up unimagined possibilities and offers a chance for rethinking

planned debate format if the participating candidates want to block all critical questions in advance? The exceptional situation here becomes an opportunity to question things and get back on track. Thus, what remains of the blackout is at least the insight that one's own scope of possibilities is sometimes greater than one would like to admit.

While conflicts that need to be dealt with are often swept under the rug in everyday life, the blackout thus becomes a catalyst for dealing with previously unspoken problems, an occasion for open discussion – and thus an opportunity to re-think one's previous dysfunctional habits and relationships, ideally to renew them. In *Grey's Anatomy's* first blackout episode (S02E05), for example, the unfamiliar situation forces important life decisions. After enduring the crisis at the power-less hospital, divorce papers are finally signed so that chief resident Derek can start a new life with title character Meredith, and Christina struggles to steady her previously casual relationship. In the blackout episode sealing season 9 (S09E24), in turn, there are more breakups than matings after the disaster experience: because secrets well hidden in the dark (such as an intimate encounter in the break room) can only be kept until the light comes back (because then, for instance, the switched T-shirts reveal the secret). After a horizon-expanding operation in the dark, Christina realizes that she already finds the fulfillment (her partner Owen hopes for in a family with her) in her job, so she

Unspoken conflicts come to light in power outage – require management and clarification

then sets off for Switzerland and really takes off with her career.

In the 15th *Grey* season, three elevator dramas run parallel to each other. During open-heart surgery (see above), a complicated love triangle seems to be gradually unraveling, and Meredith Grey, now widowed and still undecided, is also in the process of deciding between her two admirers. While the devil rages in the clinic, junior doctors Nico and Levi save themselves in an ambulance and have the opportunity to clarify their sexual identities in an almost psychotherapeutic conversation, which leads to a lovemaking session during working hours. Also in *Designated Survivor,* actionist chief of staff Emily and pedantic strategy consultant Lyor get to know a new side of each other during their forced break in the elevator, when they share traumatizing childhood experiences and Emily is able to overcome her reluctance through empathy. The list of these cathartic anecdotes could be continued at will – in any case, everything is always different between people after the blackout.

Opportunity of distraction-free dialogue offers chance to strengthen social relations

While *Grey's* colleagues are still able to cope with the blackouts, others are threatened by naked chaos. The name of the series *Code Black* (USA 2015–2018) says it all: in the underfunded and (even *with* electricity) constantly overburdened Angel's Memorial in Los Angeles, which is characterized by poor neighborhoods, the exceptional situation actually occurs every day. There are always more patients than can be properly cared for.

Exchange of experience between regular operations and disaster medicine needed to better manage crises together

When in the promisingly titled episode "Exodus" (S02E11) the entire city falls victim to a blackout and (you guessed it) the clinic's generator doesn't start, the employees are already used to the "overload" of their daily routine, so to speak. Because the medication refrigerator can only be opened electronically, it is smashed to bits, bedridden patients are carried up the stairs to the operating rooms with their last ounce of strength, and patients are triaged as if they had never done anything else. The situation is, of course, untenable, but in order to transfer the patients to a hospital with a power supply, it takes 300 ambulances to squeeze through the traffic chaos. In the hospital, which is better off financially, some doctors find it difficult to adjust to the new situation and to make correct diagnoses under high pressure. While the colleagues at Angel's Memorial, due to their constant overload situation, perceive the power blackout as a logical extension of their familiar everyday madness and simply carry on as before, the comparatively well-equipped doctors at the alternative hospital, who are 'spoiled' by orderly regular operations, are totally overwhelmed by the situation. At the end of the day, they can consider themselves lucky that their colleagues, who are familiar with *Code Black*, do not shy away from unconventional methods and, if necessary, perform life-saving operations in an examination room: "You're all insane. And you're very good at what you do." – "Yes, we are. But let's never do that again." (M34) Because the usual rules of normal operation in a hospital do not have much in common with disaster medicine, more intensive preparation of hospital staff with the laws and procedures during a serious disaster would be important.

Naturally, fire departments are particularly affected by power outages – and so are their equivalents in TV entertainment. In the episode "Tonight's The Night" (S02E13), the firefighters of *Chicago Fire* (USA 2012–) have to fight on many "fronts" at the same time. Because those affected quickly begin to freeze in the cold winter night in the often poorly insulated U.S. homes, they try to help themselves with stoves and fireplaces – which can fast lead to carbon monoxide poisoning, such as when the chimney is clogged, the furnace is defective or there is insufficient ventilation. More and more exhausted citizens come to the fire station, but the facility is not prepared to provide hot meals for hundreds of people. Provisionally, they put together an emergency supply by locating one among the many closed stores willing to let them have some canned soups. When the owner is stabbed during the looting of the store, the fireman who happens to be there – since there is no first aid kit and no emergency calls can be made – has to improvise quickly, using plastic bags as disposable gloves, kitchen rolls as bandages, vodka to disinfect and duct tape to put pressure on the wound. At the station, not only do people get hungrier and hungrier, but the children get more and more impatient. Because they are terribly bored, the

Fire departments overwhelmed in multiple roles as emergency shelter, soup kitchen and rescue – constant improvisation reaches limits already busy firefighters put on a little entertainment program (see fig. 7). When the generator fails, patience and technical expertise are needed to prevent the tense situation from escalating. Although the dedicated firefighters are willing and able to improvise to the ever new challenges, the danger that people will come to avoidable harm constantly increases with each new makeshift solution.

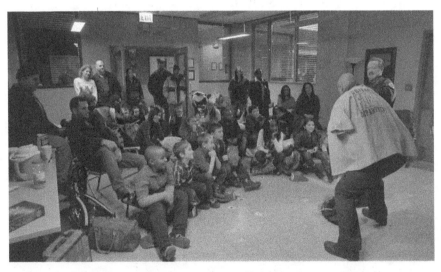

Figure 7: During the blackout in a Chicago neighborhood, Chicago Fire*'s station (S02E13M29) becomes a drop-in center for those seeking help. Here they can warm up, rest on one of the quickly set-up cots, fortify themselves with a hot meal, and for a moment also relinquish responsibility for the exhausted children who are enjoying the impromptu fire department's show.*

Even more intense is the stress that awaits the "Seattle Firefighters" at their *Station 19* (USA 2018–) in the episode "The Dark Night" (S02E13). In an apartment building affected by a power outage, the firefighters find a little girl locked in a washing machine when they suddenly smell gas – which does not go well at all with the many candles. The helpers evacuate the building while putting themselves in great danger trying to free the girl. Interestingly, the fire and police teams split into teams of two to work more closely together: one police officer and one firefighter go through the house together in order to be able to intervene more quickly and competently in an emergency. They find a resident in need of care who must be resuscitated because the equipment for his intensive care at home has failed due to the power outage. The daughter saves her father by performing persistent chest compressions. This allows her to bridge the time until the paramedics arrive, who recharge the equipment with a mobile battery and turn it back on – even though, as it then turns out, it is probably time to say goodbye. Despite the great chaos, the firefighters fulfill the dying gentleman's final wish to go in the presence of his daughter with a view of the (in this powerless dark night quite clear) starry sky. "Firefighters are taught to find our way in the dark" (M38), the main heroine tells us of her job – but to do so, firefighters must repeatedly make difficult and momentous trade-offs and decisions that always remain compromises in the confusion of an emergency situation. A resilient

Preventable emergencies, lack of civil crisis preparedness and shortage of materials make work more difficult – cooperation between police and fire departments beneficial population that behaves correctly during such events and thus prevents avoidable emergencies from occurring in the first place, as well as adequate equipment with material reserves, can at least provide some relief and appropriate, largely safe working conditions under these conditions.

When nothing else helps, the superheroes are called upon, and they have a lot to do these days. While ordinary mortals, overwhelmed by the situation, don't know what to do, the superhuman comic figures are always there and know exactly what needs to be done, such as *The Flash,* who in the episode "Power Outage" (S01E07) has to fight a villain who feeds on electricity from the public grid. Of course, Superman also comes into play, and in the episode "Operation Blackout" (S02E06) of *Lois & Clark: The New Adventures of Superman* (USA 1993–1997) he has to fight against a techno-pessimistic eco-terrorist who wants to destroy the modern world with the help of a hacked satellite. Of course, the native Kryptonian in the iconic full-body stretch suit with red cape will ascend into the sky in time to render the death satellite harmless. Until then, he must maintain his fake identity at the Daily Planet, which has also been hit by computer failures. As computers and phones stop working in the newsroom, philosophical thoughts rise in the characters about civilization's dependence on technology and the desocializing effects of mass communications. While Lois sees a "world of possibilities" in the 500 television channels, for example, Clark criticizes that the consequence of

> Power outage makes dependence on modern technology clear – but no one can do without it

television will be "that you may never again speak
to another human being" (M12). While Lois orders
a pizza by fax (!), Clark enumerates to her: "Just
look at your trip back here: you get money from the
ATM, you pay for your gas at the pump, you use
your security card to get into your underground
parking, and you did not interact with another
human being the whole time." (M13) Perhaps the
little time out will do well to demonstrate to this
'retro' 90s society – which, from today's perspective, is stuck in its technological teens – the benefits
and problems of modern civilization that are often
no longer even consciously perceived.

For the newspaper publisher, these mind games
are luxury problems: here, without electricity, some
things don't work at all and many things are much
slower than usual. When the computers stop running, typing has to be done on typewriters and
revisions made with correction fluid, and because
the telephones don't work, time-consuming on-site
appointments have to be made. Fortunately, "the
old linotype machine" still works, which is loaded
by the hard-of-hearing type setter. In fact, when the
electricity is gone in the whole city (just a diver-
sionary maneuver by the terrorists), the popular
"Daily Planet" is the only newspaper that still
appears in the morning and can supply the
population with urgently needed information –
thanks to the good old printing press, which also
works without electricity. "Guess it's gonna take
more than a few terrorists to keep this paper down,"
Lois sums up at the end of another 'world rescue'

Professions reflect
on their core
competencies to
deliver good work
even during power
outages

(M44). Apparently, what's needed most in times of a power outage are people who are willing to just keep doing what they do best at the time – even under difficult conditions.

4. ATTACK ON MODERNITY: BLACKOUT TERRORISM AND CRIMINALITY

Often, there is no malicious intent behind power failures in thematically relevant feature films and series episodes: usually it is a chain of unfavorable coincidences, at worst a rather thoughtless negligence (cf. chapter 3). Strikingly, however, the blackout in film and television does not always come across as innocent, on the contrary: especially in recent years, such scenarios are on the increase, in which the blackout is intentionally caused, either by terrorists out of ideological conviction, or by criminals who want to enrich themselves – and regularly the boundaries between both motives become blurred. Their attack is aimed at the modern way of life, which is either to be fought as the cause of undesirable effects such as climate change, or as a means of pressure to extort a personal advantage. In either case, the consequences of the induced blackout are so drastic that modern society usually retaliates with all the means at their disposal – as long as they are still able to do so without electricity at all.

Criminal and terrorist attacks on power supply are fought with all means of the rule of law

In his novel *Blackout – Tomorrow Will Be Too Late* ([2012]2017), German science fiction author Marc Elsberg showed how difficult it is for a modern world to defend itself against its enemies when it is practically incapacitated by the loss of its lifeblood. Here, Europe and the U.S. are hit by a devastating two-week blackout organized by a radical anti-globalization terrorist group, fighting modern technology and elites as 'gravediggers' of humanity and the environment. By striking at the electrified civilization, the rather arbitrary bunch of far-left and far-right fanatics from the better-off middle class hopes to be able to force a transformation of society according to their (ultimately unclear and rather confused) ideas. In fact, however, it is precisely the poorest and weakest who are hit hardest by a blackout, because the public services that are particularly important for them then no longer function and they cannot prepare for such a situation as easily as the wealthy.

People who have neither money for elaborate crisis precautions nor for expensive speculative goods are most dependent on government aid, which, however, cannot be provided in the event of such a cross-border emergency: because every individual is directly affected by the crisis and every government first wants to get a grip on the situation in its own country, no help from others or support from outside can be expected in the medium to long term. In the book, hundreds of thousands die due to lack of medical treatment, the interrupted drinking water supply, food shortages and from hypothermia, in traffic accidents and in violent crimes. In 800 pages, Elsberg tells a thriller in search of the perpetrators of this mass-murderous hack against modernity, which is to be brought to a standstill, perhaps even to its demise. The gifted computer geek Manzano becomes the hero (with the support of the tirelessly reporting journalist Shannon), who gets on the trail of the criminals with ever new technical

Public services collapse in the event of a blackout, as no outside help can be requested

114

tricks, for which the investigating authorities lack the imagination. Until then, however, incidents in inadequately cooled nuclear power plants, prison breaks and even government coups accumulate – the collapse of Western modernity can only be stopped at the last moment, if at all.

While in the book it is left to one's own ingenuity to picture the catastrophic consequences of terror, the recent German television series *Blackout* (2021), based on Elsberg's novel, finds vivid images for the ensuing chaos. The series places the character of crisis staff chief Frauke Michelsen (passionately embodied by Marie Leuenberger) at the center of the plot, tilting at windmills with her demand for a rapid massive expansion of disaster relief in the German Federal Ministry of the Interior. Time and again, politicians try to talk down the problem so as not to expose themselves to accusations of loss of control at the next election (which, of course, has the opposite effect) and rely on the arbitrary information from the grid operators that the power will be back in just a few hours. When, as Michelsen predicted as a worst-case scenario, electricity still doesn't flow after days, the dimensions of such a national catastrophe gradually become visible: because 462 generators in a country of 83 million people are not even enough to supply the most important facilities – the 'critical infrastructures' ("KRITIS") such as the police, water supply and authorities as well as emergency shelters, nursing homes and prisons – with emergency power, public order collapses in a picture-perfect manner within a very short time.

Committed crisis managers vs. appeasing politicians – but blackout requires immediate action

The anarchic images that the series finds for this may not be particularly imaginative, but they are remarkable for German television, which still has some catching up to do with disaster narratives compared to Hollywood. However, in the series *Blackout*, the filmic disaster comes to life: tanks roll through the sparsely lit government district to keep the hungry and thus angry demonstrators at bay; supermarkets are emptied or looted, the federal food emergency reserve is depleted, people shoot each other out of fear and over trifles in knee-jerk reactions; caregivers no longer show up for work, leaving those in need of help to fend for themselves, and those who can no longer be helped are made to face inevitable death with as little pain as possible; garbage piles up in the streets and a weeks' worth of feces stands in the toilets, morgues are overflowing, epidemics loom... After only eight days, as the series tells us and, above all, visualizes, the Federal Republic would effectively (and this is to be understood literally) be at the *end* without outside help.

> Devastating consequences of attack quickly create disturbing images of state's and society's overburdening

Obviously, a blackout is an extremely unfavorable instrument for eliminating social grievances, as even the terrorists themselves must admit. In general, more can be learned about the motives of the pseudo-revolutionaries in the television series than in the book, because it adds a remarkable plot line to the novel narrative. In Elsberg's book, the restless Manzano (just as the other characters are somewhat naïve, or at least stereotypical, about some professions) is simply a gifted computer geek who, because of his special skills, gets caught between the wheels

> Anarchists want to force rethinking with blackout – but create only suffering and resistance

of the technically overburdened investigating authorities – but ultimately stands as a hero because he
apprehends the culprits, deciphers their tricks, and
is able to end the blackout. In the series, on the
other hand, the police's suspicion that the Italian-
born expert himself might have had something to
do with the crime, given his amazing knowledge, is
not unfounded. As is revealed in the course of the
episodes, Manzano was not exactly averse to anarchist ideas in his wild political youth. When he and
his comrades-in-arms demonstrated against the G8
in Genoa in 2001, where there was arbitrary police
violence, they came up with a plan to 'really make a
difference': young Manzano proudly tells of the
code he smuggled in during a programming gig,
which can be used to switch on and off the 'intelligent' electricity meters of private households en
masse at will. One is overcome by the idea of giving
Europe a 'lesson': "When people are sitting in the
dark, they might start to think a bit about what is
important in life. Whether it's right that the rich are
getting richer and richer and that we're ruining our
planet right now. We need a restart!" (S01E03M28;
own translation) It's probably not just youthful
overzealousness, but also the constant drug-induced
clouding of consciousness that causes hardly anyone
in the group to spot the gaps in the plan (one thinks
it's all "absurd science fiction" (S01E03M27; own
translation). The group breaks up when some of
them are imprisoned and tortured, while Manzano
makes a deal with the authorities, testifies against
his friends, and is released. Manzano is a traitor to

them, and apparently some have now put his fantasy into action. The series makes it plausible why Manzano, of all people, feels called to get to the bottom of the matter: out of justified feelings of guilt for being potentially responsible for the deaths of countless people (see fig. 8).

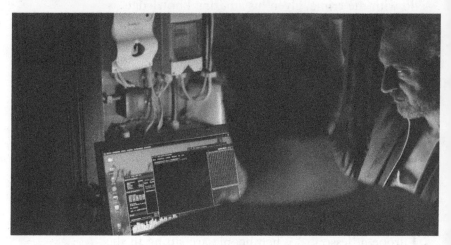

Figure 8: "Today you have to be an engineer to understand these things," complains the somewhat too clichéd but good-natured Italian about the digital 'smart' electricity meters when Moritz Bleibtreu's character in the Joyn series Blackout *(S01E01M16; own translation) discovers that one of his unsuccessful youthful pranks has been used by anarchists to orchestrate a Europe-wide breakdown of the power supply. It takes highly skilled (even not always innocent) computer specialists to get the system working again.*

Manzano drives off – in front of the constantly dark and foggy landscape of cinematic standard scenery – his old comrades, most of whom, however, have left their wild times behind them. The lawyer, who now occasionally represents political pro bono for the conscience, only thinks to himself:

Moderate anarchists know that blackout does not create change, but new redistribution from the poor to the rich

"Nobody can be that stupid. If we're going to save the world from global warming, it's going to be with innovation and technology, not a return to the Stone Age!" (S01E05M11; own translation) Even the clichéd snotty leftists, who have inherited and live in a pleasant loft with a self-sufficient solar energy supply on the roof, feel called to something higher than simply playing a trick on modernity: "We want to build something new here, not destroy anything. We want to create the counter-design to the neoliberal madness out there" (S01E05M25; own translation) – which is of course easy to say over expensive red wine and with rare paintings on the wall. "In the long run, maybe it's like a cleansing shower for our diseased planet," one of the ex-anarchos whitewashes the blackout and is directly rebuked by his wife: "Till, can you please stop romanticizing this blackout?" (S01E05M25; own translation) Finally, Manzano meets his former great love, with whom he once shared the political dream of a better life. Twenty years after the events in Genoa, he meets her again during the blackout in search of those responsible – and finds that she, of all people, had given away the secret of his backdoor in the smart meter program to a megalomaniac millionaire with perfidious political goals. She also tries to put the deaths of the countless into perspective: "When did really great changes take place? When were corrupt systems destroyed? Always only after a great catastrophe." (S01E06M43; own translation) Manzano, who almost perished several times during his

chase through Europe, whose in the meantime beloved Shannon fell victim to rioters and who has
seen too much suffering as a result of the blackout,
can hardly control himself: "Have you been outside
in the last few days? Have you seen what's going on?
Have you seen people croak? Have you seen them
fighting over a fucking piece of bread? ... You really
think this blackout will hurt the rich? It's the very
poorest that get hit the hardest!" (S01E06M43) In
tears, the collaborator admits that she had hoped
"after two days at the latest, the lights will come
back on" (S01E06M45; own translation) – instead,
the first season ends with the lights over Berlin going out again, after finally burning for a few hours
after a week of devastation, as the self-involved criminals have been able to escape in the meantime to
get ready for the next attack on the modern world.

Apart from the fact that it is not advisable to
have the programming of sensitive software parts
cobbled together in the form of student work contracts without further examination, some other interesting findings emerge. The terrorists are pro-
ceeding with a strategy that has been planned for
years and has multiple precautions. First, they exploit
the backdoor in smart meter devices to switch
households on and off, creating overloads and load
shedding in the power grid. Second, the terrorists are
deliberately blowing up transmission towers to
destabilize not only the virtual but also the physical
infrastructure of the power supply. The third com-
ponent, the manipulation of power plants, appears to
be the most insidious: instead of using great effort to

Terrorists choose
multiple parallel
strategies to attack
power grid –
digital, physical,
psychological

influence the production mechanisms themselves, the hack targets only the displays of the measuring instruments. The power plant employees see on the display a fault (which in reality does not exist) in the production system and then fight with inappropriate means an imaginary problem. The machines now really come to harm and fall off the grid. In doing so, the terrorists take advantage of "the biggest weak point in the system: the people" (S01E06M29; own translation), as Manzano describes it in the series. These people in the power plant, however, who can make mistakes, can also do a lot of things right, such as the technicians in the nuclear power plant who work tirelessly and at the risk of their lives, waiting until the last second for the fuel to save them instead of making a run for it, despite the threat of a melt-down. While the systems gradually go crazy without cooling and radioactive gas threatens to escape, they fight on site with the machines and with the government for a truckload of diesel to still avert the 'maximum credible accident' ("GAU"). "You all are setting a good example for all of us," a member of the local administration praises the gentlemen and hands them a satellite phone "with best wishes from the crisis team in Berlin" (S01E05M37; own translation) – because if you want to do something in a blackout, you need a means of communication that is armed against any malicious intent by terrorists and hackers.

Even crisis team leader Michelsen has to watch with her own eyes how the world is gradually going down without her being able to do anything about it. As the person responsible for a disaster control

Blackout creates overload for responsible parties due to undecidable dilemmas

exercise with a blackout scenario, she had pointed out the risks, but went unheard. Now she is not only burdened by the fact that countless people are dying in an avoidable way, but she is also worried about her children, who have disappeared since their train broke down in a forest without power and was evacuated. Although the two girls are lucky enough to be taken in by a caring man – who at first seems a bit creepy, but is actually particularly helpful – they are unreachable and thus untraceable, as there are no telephone connections anymore. The burden on the decision-maker Michelsen increases even more when the Interior Minister refuses the urgently needed offers of humanitarian aid from Russia – that could, after all, (together with China!) be behind the attack. Because there is no more reliable information, journalists cannot publish their research, and communication between the authorities is reduced to a minimum, speculations bordering on conspiracy theories gradually spread like wildfire ("Chinese secret service, or KGB, they are supposed to be behind it," S01E03M05; own translation). Michelsen, however, does not accept the hypotheses, even if they were true: "We are finished!", because after a little over a week without power supply a situation has arisen where people simply starve and die of thirst in their homes, because there is hardly any private provision for crisis situations worth mentioning. Again and again, impossible decisions have to be made, for example when it comes to distributing the scarce diesel: "Babies in incubators, injured people on the operating table, dialysis patients – these people will all die!" – "If there's a reactor disaster, the hospital won't matter anymore!" (S01E04M37; own translation) Gradually, those in charge begin to despair as all their efforts seem to come to naught and every well-intentioned aid measure in the face of scarcity also implies a 'death sentence' at the same time.

One of the advantages of fictional freedom is that a catastrophe can be averted just at the right moment, but that is why it remains a fairy tale. In reality, however, it is precisely this second week of a blackout that decides whether it is still possible to return to modern living conditions in time – or whether it is already too late. Terrorists who (whether for fundamentalist, ideological or other reasons) are serious about their hatred of modern society know very well that the damage caused, as in a pandemic, grows exponentially over time – so quickly, in fact, that the damage would be almost unmanageable by the third week without electricity: when all state reserves run out, people stop showing up for work, and everyone is forced to think only of themselves and their loved ones, the complex interdependencies on which efficient modern society thrives can no longer be redeemed. When, two weeks after an attack on the power grid, police forces and fire departments are no longer operational, infrastructures are no longer maintained and administration and government no longer function, the collapse of the social contract is imminent.

> Damage from blackout grows exponentially over time – until there is nothing left

Figure 9: In The Coming Days *(M59), the sleeper cell of an anti-civilization terrorist organization sabotages the power supply to spread fear and terror and provoke an overthrow of the government. When this also causes the water to fail, the people have to wash their heads with the already scarce drinking water from the Tetra Pak – but how long will it last?*

Provoking such a state of affairs is also the perfidious plan of the "Black Storms," who in the German futuristic drama *The Coming Days* (2010) want to deal the decisive blow to the "small declining affluent democracy" (M70; own translation) with murder and bombings, provocations and, of course, hacker attacks on the Internet and thus on the hyper-networked power supply (see fig. 9). In the fictitious year 2012 – from the perspective of a script from 2010 – there are ever new resource wars for the last remaining oil reserves, escalating by the year 2020 and lead to mass impoverishment even in the industrialized countries. There is not much left of the Federal Republic of Germany: the streets are filled with tents where the countless homeless and refugees languish – but the supermarket shelves are

Energy crisis and resource war fosters rise of terrorism

empty. Only the villas of the rich are secured like fortresses and sealed off from the problems of the general population. Suffering Germany is somehow keeping its head above water by participating in the wars for the last oil, but at the same time this is attracting an unmanageable mass of refugees who are hoping to catch a small share of the remaining former consumer wealth.

While these hopeless people face ever-larger, insurmountable walls, others 'take refuge' in a self-sufficient mountain life – with a wooden house, solar cell, and goats. That this illusory idyll cannot, of course, provide a solution to the problem of the crisis of modern society, which is destroying its own livelihood, is self-explanatory, but the comparatively wealthy characters, who can afford to simply drop out of the modernization game and in turn embark on their very own 'escape', may find a little peace here from the impending collapse of Western civilization – at least as long as there is no medical emergency and no one is not dependent on the modern institutions.

Flight of the wealthy to villas and mountain huts only postpones problem to

In the Belgian series *Unit 42* (2017–), the cybercrime special unit of the Brussels police has to deal with similarly unscrupulous terrorists. In the episode "Reboot" (S01E10), a short-circuit is created in a transformer station when the political criminals use a drone to throw a metal rod into the transformer station. The motives and plans of those responsible remain unclear at first, but the consequences are all the clearer: the capital is without power because the disturbance in the individual

Law enforcement barely able to work due to blackout – analog emergency solutions required

plant causes a chain reaction of voltage spikes ("I thought the interconnection protects us?" – "The rebuttal," M04). The police themselves are also affected: without electricity and the Internet, digital files cannot be searched ("How did they do it before?" – "They convicted innocent people," M10), conversations are only possible via radios. Computers stop working because the construction site generators are not designed for the sensitive IT. In the words of one police officer: "Nowadays even the truth depends on electricity." (M04)

They get on the trail of an eco-fanatic group whose members, however, have different inhibition thresholds: while one activist films menacing cracks in nuclear power plants with his drone, pointing out safety risks (for which he was once fired as a nuclear plant employee) but shies away from acts of sabotage, the others believe that the only way to bring about change is through concrete action. Billie, a hacker who is a member of *Unité 42,* can't help but feel a certain fascination for the revolutionaries, because they don't just seem to want to expose unjust circumstances and dangerous conditions ("This story will definitely make a difference. It will rekindle the debate about the safety of energy security... The cracks, the overflights, I could really freak out... Soon we'll have Chernobyl here, and no one will care", M20), but they also seem to have unrivaled technical skills to enforce their convictions.

Blackout terrorists technically very capable and fighting for a seemingly 'just cause', therefore danger of sympathizers

It turns out that the terrorists have infected much of the computers of government agencies and critical infrastructure – including those of prisons, hospitals, and nuclear power plants – with a self-reproducing virus. The blackout ultimately served only as a means to an end, allowing the virus to be introduced while replacement systems were not yet up and running. Because the terrorists (themselves no longer the youngest) were among the first to program the security systems of computer networks at the time, they know their security vulnerabilities, especially if they are used unchanged for a long time – as is often the case in the somewhat modernization-lethargic government agencies. This is also the reason why they rely on ancient technology from the computer museum for their attacks: these are the last devices that can communicate with the old-fashioned and failure-prone systems. Finally, as planned, the worm settles down everywhere, and the forecasts are predicting devastating consequences: "Stock market crash, health catastrophe, nuclear incidents…. actually all sorts of things… Their intentions are clear: to reduce everything to rubble." (M32; own translation) The chief commissioner of the cyber unit fears the worst and gives his children iodine pills (despite the good intentions, this is not a good idea, because prophylactic treatment can cause serious side effects and must be given only as officially instructed).

Outdated technology and software becomes a gateway for hacking – especially for critical infrastructures with dramatic consequences

Figure 10: Bang or click? The terrorists in the blackout episode of Unit 42 *(S01E10M40) disagree on how far they want to go for their anarchist principles. In any case, a shot in the wrong direction would make it impossible to stop the national blackout, which can be triggered by keyboard. Then, cynically, only another blackout would help.*

The terrorists put their deadly plan into action and paralyze the country while they withdraw billions from the hacked bank systems and give them away to activists and random persons. It comes to a showdown at the Museum of Technology: "Who has more power? One finger on a command key, or one on a trigger?" (cf. fig. 10; own translation) Because starting the infiltration would provoke another domino effect infecting the entire country, only one option remains: this time, the policemen throw the metal rod into the substation themselves in order to force all devices to go offline and thus remain unharmed by a renewed blackout – even if

Ability to create a blackout demonstrates power – last resort: intentional blackout to avert hacking attack on infrastructure this means a risk for the population as long as the city is switched off again.

Terrorists don't always stay true to their 'ideals' when opportunity knocks. The *Bugs* from the British 90s series (UK 1995–1999) are called in when technical expertise at its finest is needed to catch the bad guys. The *Bugs* are also consulted for the episode "Blackout" (S02E05), when alleged environmentalists occupy the new fusion reactor and knock out the city's power grid as a show of force ("Now we have the power", M04). Because destroying the internal communication channels and overcoming the practically unprotected control rooms is child's play for the fanatics "Pro Earth Front", they can easily lend weight to their demands: the decommissioning of all isotope fissioning facilities, the rededication of the facilities for solar research, and the transfer of company profits to waste recycling research. While the operating company praises the fusion technology as "a safe, inexpensive and pollution free answer to the world's energy needs" (M01), the criminals see this as a welcome pretext for a perfidious plan: the energy 'collected' since the blackout is to be diverted by "tiny bursts of current, nano surges" (M33) into a large bank to disable its security and control systems and then rob it.

Even though this is technically all pretty nonsense, the *Bugs* still keep things exciting, because it's no longer just about a bank robbery, but leads into a nationwide blackout. The terrorists are contacted during their hostage-taking at the fusion power

> Terrorists with ostensibly ideological goals use pretexts for material enrichment

> Fanatics are also susceptible to personal gains that make them forget about political goals

plant by an arms dealer who promises them a chunk of money for sensitive fuel materials needed for safe operation, and they are easily persuaded by the deal because "even 'concerned citizens' need to make a living" (M22). With this offer they cannot refuse, the progress pessimists quickly forget why they had come in the first place. Of course, the *Bugs* manage to avert the danger at the last second (see fig. 11) and at the same time make cool remarks when the blackout ends: "Power to the people!" (M47) Even if the series lives primarily from its techno bullshit, it shows again and again that progressive technologies can pose a danger if they fall into the wrong hands and sensitive infrastructures must be sufficiently secured against foreign takeover.

It's very similar in the somewhat stale TV movie *Blackout – Terror Just Hit the Lights* (USA 2011). Here, the power outage brought about in Los Angeles is first for revenge and then for personal gain. The criminals initially try to take control of the power grid from the outside, but only succeed in interrupting the supply for a short time. Only a kidnapped programmer who had developed the operator's security system is able to maintain the blackout for a longer period of time. When the employees at headquarters notice the problem, they reset the system completely – so there's nothing left to hack. They have to take matters into their own hands on site. Unfortunately, it's almost too easy to distract the security guards and gain access to the control centers – where the employees feel forced to exe-

Blackout as a means for criminals to gain access to secured systems (e.g. banks)

cute the criminals' shutdown commands at gun-point (see. fig. 12). Interestingly, the manipulation and eventual hostile takeover of the power grid only succeeds through the hostage-taking and blackmail of experts from the industry – with their specialized knowledge, they are a weak point in the security system because they could relatively easily be coerced into causing power outages under threat of violence (against them or their loved ones). Ultimately, however, it is these people in the film who ultimately demonstrate the courage to defend themselves against the money-hungry criminals.

Figure 11: In an episode of the 90s cult series Bugs *(S02E05), eco-terrorists want to take control of a fusion reactor, but the clever trio is able to prevent a nuclear disaster literally at the last second. The control screens in computer game aesthetics make it clear to even the last viewer that every second is at stake here.*

Figure 12: In the trashy TV movie Blackout – Terror Just Hit the Light, *terrorists don't have to go to any great lengths to break into the control center of the Los Angeles regional utility: the lone guard at the barrier is easily tricked. As is so often the case in such films, a hero arrives at the last second to avert the worst – something you shouldn't count on in real life.*

In general, the blackout narratives would be impossible without the selfless heroines with their almost superhuman abilities, who in the end always ensure that the greatest catastrophe can be averted at the last second. In "Power Play" (S02E15), the cunning thief in his *White Collar* (USA 2009–2014), who helps the FBI fight crime as a substitute for a prison sentence, has to do a lot of dangerous research work to find out that the increasing power outages in New York are connected to speculation on the electricity market: artificial shortages are manipulating the price of electricity to make it pay off

Heroic experts help law enforcement fight blackout causes

handsomely for the criminals. In the episode "De-crypt" (S04E10) of the series *The Good Doctor* (USA 2017–), blackmailers encrypt the computer system of a hospital and endanger the lives of count-less people. The hospital director wants to give in and pay the demanded sum (after all, you don't want to have your insurance rates for such cases transferred for nothing), but the clever IT expert knows how to clean up the system and save the hos-pital's infrastructure. It even turns out that the 'hackers' were just bluffing when they threatened to infect expensive diagnostic equipment.

A combination of physical strength and brains is required when organized crime sabotages a re-cently completed giant skyscraper by disabling all automatic fire safety systems to remove evidence of tangled money laundering operations. *Skyscraper* (USA 2018) Dwayne Johnson must prevent a 'Tow-ering Inferno' in order to save his family. To do so, he jumps from a crane jib onto the burning building at a height of hundreds of meters and fights his way to his daughter – armed only with a roll of duct tape with which he can solve any problem. Meanwhile, his wife gets her hands back on the tablet stolen by the criminals, which would be used to control the systems – if the crooks' IT guy hadn't encrypted and compromised everything. Aware that her husband and daughter are still holding out in the burning high-rise, she quickly grasps the problem and clicks on "Reboot": the good old trick of switching your computer off and on again when it goes haywire

Poorly secured systems as a gateway for sabotage – remote reboot as a last resort to restart hacked systems also works on the billion-dollar house in self-destruct mode. Obviously, entrusting the security of such a building to a single tablet is a fire hazard. Fortunately, there are again particularly capable and fearless characters who spoil the fun for the greedy gangsters. They don't always have a 'clean slate' themselves, but have outstanding abilities to solve a complex problem like an artificially generated power outage before it's too late.

The villains in cinematic blackout narratives are usually concerned either with the 'big picture', with upsetting social conditions, or with making quick easy money. Somewhat more trivial are the motivations that drive the perpetrator of the power cut in "Mr. Monk and the Blackout" (S03E03). In the series about the obsessive-compulsive but highly gifted Detective *Monk* (USA 2002–2009), San Francisco is repeatedly hit by city-wide blackouts because generators at the power plant are blown up at night. The criminal tries to cover up one's track by leaving a faked 'letter of confession'. The author of the note is identified as a convicted terrorist who had already blown up army installations 10 years ago; he didn't have much to do with climate issues then. The trail seems to go nowhere, as the suspect had committed suicide shortly before his trial at that time – at least apparently. Only a tree-hugger puts them back on the right track: when he hears that his former best friend is responsible for the deaths of two heart patients and a dialysis patient by causing the blackout, he contacts him – obviously the killer's

Banal personal motives for attack on power supply – always murderous because of fatal consequences

demise was just a staging. The environmental reasons are only pretended, instead the terrorist only cares about his own skin: because the country music lover was unexpectedly filmed by television during a concert, he feared that his false identity would be exposed should someone recognize him during the broadcast – which is why he unceremoniously shuts down the power supply at the exact moment when the broadcast (and then the replay) is aired. This time, Monk is also directly affected, stuck in the elevator with his date (as he feared). For the order-loving Monk, the blackout is of course a burden, because it means loss of control and experiences of insecurity, which he compensates for by the typical compulsive repetition of words promising protection ("Lobby, lobby, lobby...," S03E03M27). For future blackouts, the resourceful detective acquires a night vision device, which he actually uses to almost outsmart the killer who visits him at home in the dark. However, the plan with the night vision device has a catch: you have to find it in the dark first.

Characters who cause blackouts are hardly sympathetic: they accept the death of innocent people. The only ones who can perhaps be forgiven for not knowing how to help themselves other than by blacking out their city are the replicants in the hyperelectrified world of *Blade Runner*, the dark, constantly rainy Los Angeles from the 1982 cyberpunk film starring Harrison Ford. A short film made in conjunction with the sequel Blade *Runner 2049* (USA 2017) bridges the gap between the two parts.

Science fiction: blackout as a means of liberation from oppressive rule

Blade Runner Black Out 2022 (USA/JP 2017) focuses on the perspective of the replicants, these particularly human-like and powerful robots. Since these are hardly to be distinguished from their fleshy creator, but in the meantime substantially more clever and strong than their human models, the 'real' people make hunt for their improved copies. In order to recognize the perfect human imitations, they use a database of the manufacturer, in which all replicants are registered. For the machines, it's all about 'survival': "We may live longer, but life doesn't mean living. ... No heaven or hell for us. This world is all we got." (M10) They plan an uprising against the oppressive system by destroying the database. For this purpose, the bomb is to be detonated directly over Los Angeles during a nuclear missile test, so that the resulting 'electromagnetic pulse' (EMP) shuts down all devices and deletes electronic data; in addition, an explosion is to destroy the servers physically as well. From one moment to the next, under the mushroom cloud, the millions of lights in the small windows of the dark facades disappear, the flying cabs so typical of this world fall through the deep canyons between the skyscrapers and crash into the iconic garish billboards (see. fig. 13).

With the great blackout, many will lose their lives – but anonymity guarantees the surviving replicants a new freedom at the same time. Those who do not experience modernity as a place of fulfillment and develop hatred against it and its isolating mechanisms will probably be ready for any fight. Unfortunately, a blackout is one of the most efficient ways to fight this battle. Modernity should not only be afraid of the always feared 'usual suspected' terrorists and the ruthless criminals, but must also reckon with the hopeless lonely ones who experience modern life as not worth living and have nothing to lose. Only when everyone feels they have a fair share in the successes and wonders of modernization will it remain worth protecting for everyone.

Not only terror and greed, but also alienation and loneliness can become dangerous for modernity

Figure 13: The replicants from Blade Runner Black Out 2022 (M13) *no longer want to be bullied by humans and want to disappear into anonymity in May 2022 by means of a blackout. In doing so, they also accept that the hypertechnical Los Angeles with its computer-controlled machines will collapse.*

5. NOW EVERYTHING WILL BE DIFFERENT: ON THE ROAD TO POST-MODERNITY

In all the films and series discussed so far, the blackout leads to serious consequences, but it ultimately remains temporary and localized – a brief interlude that interrupts the usual life, but as such cannot really call it into question. But when blackouts occur in cinematic art forms, they are much more often an omen that something is very wrong, that modernity is facing fundamental problems that will perhaps no longer be easily solved, that perhaps even the transition to a *post*-modern epoch has begun. The blackout then becomes a threshold experience, the experience of an 'in-between', between 'no longer' modernity and 'not yet' post-modernity. The sudden de-electrification and its harbingers thereby become for the characters an unmistakable sign of the fading of the accustomed modern reality of life. Only if they can recognize and interpret the clues in time, they will be able to survive this transition and then settle into the new electricity-free world. Otherwise, they will be left behind in an era that has long since passed.

The end of the modern age rarely comes without notice in disaster and doomsday films. Often the blackout is one of the clearest omens: it has a signaling effect for the beginning termination of the previous normality. But the end of the electric age is also usually announced in advance – one only has to

Blackout announces itself for a long time in film and television – but signs must be recognized and classified

recognize the (not always very obvious) signs in time and act accordingly. How does this process manifest itself and how do the characters deal with it? How do the protagonists of these fictional worlds know whether they are dealing with a temporary power outage, or a widespread blackout of uncertain duration? What are the typical reasons for this threatening regression to pre-modern times or the exceeding of the life expectancy of modernity? And is there still hope that life will go on in this new world? This chapter is devoted to the manifold cinematic-televisual causes that lead to such blackouts that make everything different, and looks at the various signs that herald it.

The variety of blackout scenarios ranges from climatic changes and other ecological crises, astronomical events and failed scientific experiments, (digital or conventional) warfare and electromagnetic pulses (EMPs) to the attack of aliens and zombies. Obviously, there are many ways to de-electrify the modern world, which are only facilitated by a dilapidated infrastructure, lack of crisis preparedness by the state and households, and irrational individual behavior.

Blackout causes: climate, astronomy, experiments, war, EMP, aliens, zombies

The most credible and urgent scenarios seem to be the blackout narratives, in which questions of resource scarcity and geopolitical tensions are brought into focus. In the French mini-series *L'Effondrement* (*The Collapse*, 2019), serious changes loom in a very present future. On the television screens of this fictional world, there are rather realistic programs

Escalation stages of collapse: bad news, empty shelves, flickering lights, dry gas stations...

about deforestation of the rainforests, factory live-stock farming, military demonstrations of power, plastic in the oceans – and a so-called 'collap-sologist' who gains access to an otherwise fairly un-exciting talk show to spread his message of coming doom: "We're about to witness the collapse of our civilization, and I can tell you: no institution in this world is prepared for what's coming." (S01E01M02; own translation) In eight episodes, the series tells of this gradual collapse, from the first omens to the bitter end. Initially, everything still seems relatively normal. In the supermarkets, peo-ple stand patiently in the queues for their weekend shopping and somehow everything is there, but somehow also not: the shelves are full, but the tam-pons are out, also chocolate cream and ground beef are out of stock ("We still have this vegan meat, yes, but no one buys that...", S01E01M06; own translation) – there are simply no more supplies coming in since the great gasoline shortage, not even leftovers for the homeless man. The gaps in the shelves are unusual, but not really dangerous, no one would have to starve as long as they accept to live without their chocolate cream. Again and again, the lights keep going out for a few seconds, sometimes a few minutes, the card payment and ATM machines don't work, which is especially inconvenient for panic buying. Only a week later, the mood tips and the panic grows faster and faster, because the fuel shortage becomes more and more threatening: at the gas stations, you can only pay with groceries now – 500 euros for a can of gasoline is simply too little in this fictional world, in which money will soon be worth nothing anyway. When the gas pumps don't give a drop more, the situation escalates: already in the second episode, everyone thinks only of themselves, for the last canned goods and running cars they are ready for anything – even if this can only delay the decline, but not stop it.

The rich have of course made provisions for this situation. When the yellow satellite phone rings in the third episode, the owner of a very special insurance product is told to come to the airfield as quickly as possible: "The implementation of the security plan was decided tonight" (S01E03M03; own translation) – even if it remains unclear exactly what this 'plan' consists of. In any case, the electricity is now gone: the vacuum cleaner does not work anymore. The decadent mansion owner becomes hectic: he leaves everything behind, including the frightened mistress, for whom there is of course no room either in the limousine or in the rescuing airplane, but he prefers to take the Van Gogh with him, even if it costs valuable time. At the airport there are already the cabriolets and sports cars of the other policyholders who have been left behind with their keys in the ignition – he is too late. The simpler people can only dream of such a chance to escape: they have to see for themselves where they will stay. In the countryside, some are trying to reorganize themselves, for example by setting up council-led communities. Unfortunately, no one here can contribute much more than the few canned goods from their backpacks, because a month after

The wealthy have the opportunity to make extensive crisis provisions – the poor are largely left to their own means

the collapse, the former job as a printer supplies salesman no longer counts for much; only the doctor is held in high esteem here. Among the far too many new applicants for the democratically organized residential community are only a carpenter and a midwife; the others who are 'useless' for postmodern life would probably have to be fed. No wonder that the well-intentioned concept does not work out: during the attempt of the obviously 'superfluous' to seize the supplies and medicines, someone dies. The project of a new life in the dark times after the blackout is finished before it has really begun.

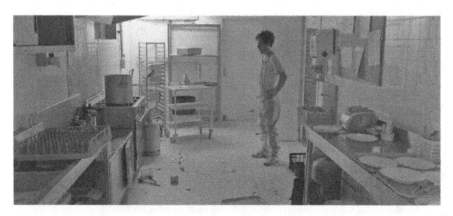

Figure 14: Even after the titular Collapse *(S01E06M11), a caretaker at a senior citizens' facility doesn't want to abandon those in need of help. But when even the last pitiful scraps of food are stolen, he finds himself forced to euthanize them in order to spare the residents, who are already in pain, an agonizing death from starvation.*

From here on, it is clear that the further un-winding of the modernization will not be stopped. The characters have ignored the warning signs and have walked into an open knife. In episode 5, a month and a half has already passed since the black-out. Just with buckets of water from a river, volun-teers are trying with their last ounce of strength to cool an overheated nuclear power plant left behind – the reactors can't just be shut down. But the system is already boiling, and the holdout slogans no longer work: meltdown looms, and with it the contamination of the entire region. Evacuation is no longer possible, with what and to where should you evacuate in this situation? In a nursing home, only one caregiver is left, with too many bedridden and too little food and painkillers – he sees no other way out, and neither do the sick: "It's the end of a world. A good time to go." (S01E06M17; own translation; cf. fig. 14) Finally, it explains where the upper class has dispersed to: just like the belated millionaire, the national environment minister has also bought the ticket for an island secured with armed drones and heavy boat locks. However, whether they will really be able to sit out the transition to the post-electric age in their hermetically sealed commune of the 'prepper bourgeoisie' remains uncertain.

Melting nuclear plants, abandoned nursing homes: transition to the post-electric age painful

The characters have thus finally arrived in the post-modern era, of which the 'collapsologist' on television had warned – but it is already too late here for a turnaround toward a sustainable economy that is not based on consumption-oriented growth: counter-modernization has already taken over. Such

After a certain point, liquidation of modernization can no longer be stopped – warning signs must be recognized in time

economic and ecological crises, leading first to blackout and then to post-modernity, have often been seen in film and television, but rarely does a film or series devote itself to the process of decay in such detail. Nevertheless, the blackout in fiction never sets in from one moment to the next: it announces its coming and its severity. In this, the series *L'Effondrement* follows a typical pattern in blackout scenarios, according to which the impending doom first cautiously reveals itself, then creeps into the normality of life, becomes more and more obvious, and finally strikes with all its force. The prototypically recurring escalation stages of the blackout – the first reports on television, the cancelled flights and trains, the traffic chaos and general unrest, the emptying supermarkets and pharmacies, the empty gas pumps and finally the silencing of the radios – are so universal in their consequences that it can be pointedly said: only those characters who recognize the warning signs in time and act responsibly have at least a chance in the blackout fictions of surviving the crisis and the impending transition to post-modernity.

Before getting down to the nitty-gritty, however, the films and series usually take enough time in the exposition to contrast the impending catastrophe (for which the viewer has switched on the TV) with a functional modern reality of life: in the beginning, everything is usually still good, life provides joy and is exuberant – which only makes the end times that then follow seem even more misera-

1st stage:
The normal modern everyday life – as a contrast to the coming state of emergency

ble. Admittedly, the occasional flickering lights already occasionally let disaster shine through normality, but all in all, there is still no reason to worry, on the contrary: for the characters, the motto is *carpe diem*. In the pilot episode of the zombie series *The Walking Dead* (USA 2010–2021) with the not coincidental episode title "Days Gone Bye", there is a brief foretaste of what lies ahead in the next eleven seasons in the first few minutes, but then we directly get a nostalgic look back to the bygone modern era: Sheriff Rick sits on patrol with his deputy and best buddy Shane, philosophizing about the differences between men and women (the latter would never turn off the lights and thus accelerate climate change...), ruminating on marital problems and taking a hearty bite into a generously packed burger with really greasy fries. Modernity can be so nice – as long as there are no car chases and shootings: on his last assignment as a police officer, Rick is seriously injured and falls into a coma. When he wakes up a few weeks later, civilization has already evaporated: there are no more nurses and doctors, instead biting undead populate the corridors (here only the battery-operated emergency lighting still works), the parking lot has been converted into a repository for the dead. Rick is lucky to be picked up by two good-natured survivors among the zombies and can fortify himself with a portion of beans by candlelight – but the days of luscious burgers are clearly over. It's much the same in *A Quiet Place: Part II* (USA 2020), which begins by telling the prequel to the first part: in the small American picture book town, all is still right with the world as the father of a family does some quick shopping before going to his son's baseball game. Citrus fruits, mineral water and toys are easily snatched from the shelves as they pass by. On the field, the youngsters give their best, the proud parents in the audience cheer, there is a popular festival atmosphere – but the radio is already crackling, the dogs are barking and the ominous comet-like object appears in the sky, announcing the arrival of the conflict-loving aliens.

The invasion begins abruptly, although there were already the first quiet warning signs: in the supermarket, the cashier can't tear himself away from the television set, where reports of an alleged bomb and mass panic are being broadcast – but that's hardly something special, even under modern conditions, unfortunately. The TV news in *War of the Worlds* (USA 2005) seems more sinister. Since his divorce, dockworker Ray (Tom Cruise) feels a distance to his children, but apart from these quite typical modern everyday problems, the easygoing young man can't really complain about his life, even the workers' union makes sure he keeps his rest hours so he can spend time with his children. The son doesn't want to do homework or play baseball, but he prefers to watch TV: between silly disaster movies and commercials there are reports of power failures and earthquakes in the Ukraine and Japan caused by electromagnetic pulses – until Dad comes into the room with his baseball glove and turns off the TV. They should have kept watching instead of

2nd stage: Accumulating disaster news on television and radio

arguing in the backyard, because shortly thereafter, lightning begins to strike New York as well – the refrigerator, telephones, even wristwatches no longer work. Shortly thereafter, the streets break open, the aliens do their destructive day's work, and modernity is at an end.

The carefree existence of disaster movies and series quickly tips over into end-time anarchy, but this does not fall from a clear sky. At least the characters wouldn't have to be too surprised by the coming blackout if they took the radio coverage seriously. Unlike the hard-to-verify and gimmicky posts on social networks, which often still briefly preempt journalistic reports, television and radio news can be given some credence; at the very least, they do a good job in blackout movies and series as the first reliable early warning system – often activated even before any damage has occurred. In *10 Cloverfield Lane* (USA 2016), it is the disturbing radio reports of increasing blackouts in the country's metropolises that prompt the shady prepper Howard (embodied by 'Fred Flintstone' John Goodman) to immediately head for his eerily homely bunker. In this case, the over-caution has apparently paid off, as an alien invasion is indeed imminent, with widespread power outages making themselves known. Also the frightened people of *Into the Night* (BE 2020–) learn at the airport from the news of a mysterious mass death, whose causes remain unclear at first. The soldier Terenzio, determined to do anything, buys a seat from Brussels to New York – the main thing is that the plane goes

3rd stage: Horror stories in the media intensify

west. But when the newscaster then bangs her head on the desk while the show is on the air and, according to reports, people simply drop dead at dawn, the camouflaged man doesn't want to wait any longer: he hijacks the first plane he can find to flee from the sun, which no longer seems to be providing life on Earth, but destroying it. Something must have gone wrong with the regular change of the solar magnetic field, the passengers speculate about dangerous gamma radiation, as it is released by millions of neutron bombs. The abductees are suddenly the rescued ones, but it will hardly be possible to escape from the sun for all eternity...

Figure 15: The departure board at airports and train stations has, as here in How It Ends *(M13), an iconic significance in disaster films and especially in blackout fictions. While the emergency power supply is still running, the mass switching from "On Time" to "Delayed" to the ominous red "Cancelled" announces other times. Now it's certainly no longer worth waiting for your flight.*

It is easy to turn a blind eye to the news on radio and television or to doubt its truthfulness, especially since the consequences still seem abstract at the moment of the report itself; after all, the catastrophe seems to be happening somewhere else. In any case, the characters often lull themselves into a false sense of security despite the terrible news, even when the newscaster runs out of the studio during the special broadcast, as in *Station Eleven* (USA 2022, S01E05M07). This changes when the impending blackout suddenly becomes quite concrete and thwarts the plans of the characters: after the inevitable horror reports, the impending apocalypse upsets the complex traffic networks and finally makes itself felt via the departure boards at airports and train stations. Whereas shortly before, flights and train journeys were predominantly displayed as being on schedule, from one moment to the next the displays change to "cancelled". This is also what happens to the main character Will in the promisingly titled Netflix doomsday road movie *How It Ends* (USA 2018): when he makes a video call to his pregnant girlfriend in Seattle before his return trip from Chicago, strange noises can be heard, the young woman only says that there is a power failure, "something is wrong, I'm scared" – finally the connection breaks down (M12). On a second try, the line goes dead. He makes his way to his flight, things escalate quite quickly from there. Even before the disturbing television news, Will sees all connections turn to red on the departure board: "Cancelled" (cf. fig. 15). The mysterious seismic activity on the U.S.

4th stage:
Crisis makes itself felt in everyday life through disruptions to traffic and logistics

West Coast reported by the newscaster becomes real. Moments later, the television broadcast breaks down – and the power is gone. The soaring fighter jets and the failure of the GPS system then actually only reinforce what the blackout has already made clear: from now on, it's all downhill: "This moment is not about waiting the power to come back on. The only thing that we can control is what we decide to do." (M16)

Even in the German TV series *Blackout,* one could still believe at first that it was a local phenomenon when the lights went out in Berlin's main train station, because everyone ultimately only sees their individual section of the problem and no longer gets any reliable information about the overall situation because the mobile network quickly fails. But if only Berlin-Mitte were actually affected by a power outage, why would all connections nationwide be canceled? The departure display, on which all connections are annulled, has more to say than the overburdened lady at the information desk, because passengers are already figuring out for themselves that this is probably not the "short-term operational disruption" that the train employee is talking about (S01E01M08; own translation). Rather, the display boards appear as an expression of the interdependent interweaving of society as a whole and, in the midst of the blackout, become an unmistakable sign that big chaos is about to begin.

Departure boards full of cancelled connections signal supra-regional problem

Time and again, the movies and series in which a blackout heralds doom follow the same pattern. In *World Warz Z,* too, everything follows the familiar

Traffic chaos on the roads thwarts everyday plans

escalation phases of the doom genre: the carefree pancake family breakfast is gradually overshadowed by the disaster news on TV ("Daddy, what's 'martial law'?" M05), which can still be smiled away, however. As they sit in the car to school, the radio news reports worldwide 'rabies' outbreaks, but fortunately there is the volume control with which the madness can be turned away. Only when the family is stuck in a traffic jam and the approaching catastrophe thus affects their concrete daily routines, a rethinking begins: police motorcycles meander frantically between the waiting cars, people become restless and finally the inevitable zombie apocalypse begins.

In the Russian multi-part *Avanpost* (*The Blackout*, RU 2020), which has been turned into a series, it is also the chaos in traffic and logistics through which the great changes announce themselves: Oleg and Olga have just met in a futuristic Moscow in a fancy hotel and have landed together in his room, when the countless busy drones – which otherwise make their rounds in an orderly fashion between the facades of the skyscrapers – suddenly stop, flash red and emit a siren signal (cf. fig. 16). Like beads strung on an invisible string, they hang in the air, not knowing where to go with themselves. What the characters cannot know at this moment yet: beyond the greater Moscow area, a mysterious blackout has shut down the electricity of the entire world – the drones apparently no longer receive orders, because the control center does not exist anymore. Even though the lights are (still) on here, Oleg realizes

Logistics come to a standstill – drones disoriented as there is no longer an internet connection

that this is not normal and reliable information is now needed. In the lobby the TV is on and the visibly worried anchorwoman reports in the evening 'Novosti': "Just now we... receive the message that... not only the contact to most cities and regions within Russia is interrupted, but... to the whole rest of the world. All telephone, radio and Internet connections seem to have been cut." (S01E01M10; own translation) By that time, the traffic chaos in the streets is already perfect, as navigation and traffic guidance systems coming from the 'cloud' no longer work.

Figure 16: In a Moscow in the not-too-distant future, the lights don't go out, but the countless drones neatly lined up suddenly stop, signaling an exceptional situation. Soldier Oleg is certain: "Seems like something serious." (Avanpost, S01E01M08) – because the rest of the world has long been in the dark.

In the blackout films and series, the image of out-of-control mobility is only heightened by the frequently served images of falling airplanes. Even if they are not directly affected by a power outage

Recurring image of the falling and crashed planes announcing the end of modernity

on the ground, of course, their systems may be sensitive to electromagnetic pulses or experience difficulties when they no longer know where to land. A zombie passenger on board can also make navigation difficult, even before the blackout kicks in. Thus, in the pilot episodes of the series *Revolution* (USA 2012–2014), *Station Eleven* (USA 2022) and also in *Avanpost*, the steel birds fall from the sky in rows. In *Fin* (*The End*, S 2012), *Awake* (USA 2021) and *The Walking Dead: World Beyond* (USA 2020–2021), on the other hand, the characters wandering through the de-energized post-modern era find only the burned-out, broken wrecks of passenger planes as cautionary ruins of a modern age that has been shut down.

For the protagonists who read the signs correctly in time and decided to act appropriately, the chances are comparatively good that they will be able to simply sit out the looming crisis and the coming blackout and thus survive without damage. In the post-apocalyptic pandemic series *Station Eleven* (USA 2022), for example, the penniless Jeevan, who is prone to panic attacks, puts one and one together: the phone call with his distraught nurse, who is battling a flood of sick people in the hospital, and the press reports of an unusually aggressive "flu" are enough warning signs for him, so that he doesn't even have to wait for the other indicators of madness typical of the genre. Quick-witted, he grabs five shopping carts – while the shelves are still as full and tidy as if no one had ever shopped in the supermarket – and packs them full

5th stage: Imminent supply shortages of food and means of payment

of non-perishable food, batteries and spirits (cf. fig. 17). Here, no one is obviously taking anything from anyone, because anyone who is not yet ill either does not yet know about the dawn of the new times – or does not want to know. The cash register shows him the proud amount of $9,423.55, plus taxes. The only thing that can go wrong now is the credit card. Swiping the card becomes the all-important moment – not because the credit limit could be too low (after all, expensive credit is easy to come by in the U.S.), but because the payment service providers may have already realized that no one is going to pay back this debt anytime soon. But the payment goes through, Jeevan is just in time, and the meter-long receipt is spat out. At the sight of it, the bewildered cashier only asks if this is "because of that thing" (S01E01M28). Jeevan's recommendation to simply go home should be warning enough for the young man at the cash register. Sometimes a sincere word and an honestly concerned facial expression probably have more effect than the worst disaster news on TV.

Even the grandfather from *Radioflash*, who is a little too well prepared for the end of the world, knows that modernity is coming to an end when a nationwide blackout won't stop. He's been expecting the apocalypse for quite some time and, of course, has stockpiled everything at home that can be put to good use when there's nothing left to buy. But prescription drugs are hard to come by for good reasons, and they have a limited shelf life anyway. His latest procurement therefore takes him to the

6th stage:
Fear of shortage of medicines

abandoned village pharmacy, and on the shopping list are: penicillin, antibiotics, ACE inhibitors – everything you can't get in the post-modern era. While another 'customer' focuses on the narcotics, the grandfather figure wants only the essentials to get through a few months together with his loved ones as healthy as possible. The drugstore is still well stocked a few hours after the start of the black-out; most people probably want to wait until the problem solves itself. Grandpa puts the money on the counter for the absent pharmacist – since it won't be worth anything tomorrow anyway.

Figure 17: Because he is one of the few who anticipates that something is coming to the modern age that it is unlikely to be able to cope with, Jeevan stocks up on three months' worth of supplies in the first episode of Station Eleven *(S01E01M26). Shortly before, in a theater performance, he had already been the first to jump up to help an actor on stage when he suffers a heart attack – he acts while the others only reach for their cell phones to record a video for social media.*

Those characters who slept through the impending end of the world and who are threatened with being caught unprepared by the coming blackout are out in the cold: they find, when it is already too late, only empty shelves and great chaos. In the U.S.-influenced genre, water bottles are the most coveted commodity, which sometimes seems a bit strange when the hectic hoarder-shoppers fight over a pack of mineral water in front of the backdrop of a beautiful deep blue freshwater lake – to buy a filter would perhaps be more sustainable than the fight for some bottles of water. Aside from canned goods and crackers, there's only one thing more coveted than water, which is essential for survival: gasoline, of course. It's hard to find a cinematic blackout without a prominent "No Gas" cardboard sign in front of the service stations, often combined with a "Cash Only" notice. Then, once the power is gone, it doesn't matter anyway if there are any fuel supplies left, because even if there were gasoline, there's no way to pump it up; the pumps are electric, after all (here, unfortunately, the movies and series aren't always entirely consistent from a technical perspective). Together with the empty supermarket shelves, the sell-out of the coveted fuel is thus an unmistakable sign of an approaching catastrophe and the imminent blackout. Even if one can feel sorry for the characters in movies and series in front of the empty shelves and overcrowded gas stations, the dried up supermarkets and gas stations at least unmistakably indicate that troubled times are ahead. However, acquiring one's emergency supplies in the eye of the

7th stage:
Lack of fuel and drinking water supply

hurricane is never a good idea; most characters abandon their frantic procurements when they are in danger of getting caught between the fistfights of the other panicking shoppers.

When the news situation is clear, the flights and trains canceled, the roads clogged, the stores emptied and people already completely unnerved, there is only one last stage of escalation left: the silencing of the radios. Up to this point, radio stations have been the only remaining reliable source of information, because when telephones and cells stop working and television news can continue to be broadcast but can no longer be received, the only thing left to keep up to date is the battery-powered radio or the one installed in the car. Radio stations are usually equipped with emergency generators and, because they require less production effort than a television studio, are more resilient in a blackout crisis and can therefore broadcast for longer. But sooner or later they reach their limits when the generators have nothing left to burn or the radio people simply don't show up for work. In disaster movies and series, the radio stations still end up serving as a transmission channel for official messages from the police, fire department and civil defense authorities. In *World War Z*, the blackout has set in without anyone noticing, because the characters are too busy fighting off their fellow citizens who have mutated into zombies. The former UN intervention expert Gerry knows that it is now time to leave the city and hide. Together with his family he finds refuge with an immigrant family, where

8th stage: Radios broadcast government emergency transmissions

there are candles, water and – a radio, where only the broadcast "at the request of the New Jersey State Police Department" (M18) is played on a continuous loop: people should stay home and stock up on food and water for up to two weeks (what, of course, ideally they would have done before the blackout set in, to avoid the undead and, more importantly, last-minute shoppers).

Also via radio, the last survivors (the actual 'Walking Dead') learn in the pilot of *The Walking Dead* that there is a well-equipped refugee camp in Atlanta, the headquarters of the Center of Disease Control and Prevention (CDC), "they told people to go there, said it would be safest" (S01E01M39). The fact that there is not much left of this at the end of the first season except a lonely researcher on the verge of a nervous breakdown cannot be blamed on the radio, on the contrary: at least the wanderers now have a destination that the group can work towards, and finally they receive new important information about the plague, as well as food, a shower and warm shelter there, because the CDC has its own energy system. This is coupled with a self-destruct mechanism: when the power finally goes out, the giant laboratory blows itself up to render the dangerous pathogens harmless before they can escape to the outside. In *The Happening* (USA/IN/FR 2008) – in which the plants of the world unite to fight back against humanity with an invisible poison – important official information is also passed on by radio after the blackout, even if the reception is miserable at times. It's surprising

Official emergency response information on the radio helps people prepare for danger and find help

why the characters keep hitting the radio when there's slight static, instead of just listening to it. At least they learn where it is still safe and which areas with particularly vindictive plants to avoid.

At some point, however, even the last rushing emergency announcements fall silent, and the silence on the airwaves becomes perhaps the most disturbing foreshadowing of post-modernity. After all the stages of escalation, the end of radio broadcasts in films and series is usually the most unmistakable sign that modernity has been written off. In the Netflix horror film *Bird Box* (USA 2018), people suddenly commit suicide when they look other suicidal people in the eye. Unfortunately, the effect also occurs via screen media, which is why TV says, "Do not go outside, avoid social media. Use radio..." (M18) – and at that moment, the TV goes off the air. No one knows exactly what's happening, they just understand: "It's an endgame." (M19) When, contrary to instructions, they do leave the house to bring in supplies, it is unforgivable that they do not at least briefly turn on the radio to check on the progress of the crisis; they do not even discuss the option. In fact, they do everything wrong in the first place that can be done wrong in this situation, and most are appropriately dead before the real blackout has even begun. The psychopathic Harold from *The Stand*, on the other hand, knows how to read the signs. The radio host, who one week is still reporting on a quarantine in a small Texas town, already knows in his next broadcast: "It certainly does look like the end: humanity

9th stage:
The silencing of the radios – but the transmissions can start again at any time

160

blinking out with a whimper" – and gives himself the bullet while the program is running (S01E01M27). For Harold, it's time to take flight, because when the radio switches off itself, it's time to expect the worst.

In the volcanic dust of *How It Ends* (USA 2018), the situation is similarly hopeless, but the characters at least keep turning the knob of the radio and try to receive a signal – five days after the start of de-electrification, unfortunately without success. Nevertheless, the radio remains the great source of hope: after grueling weeks in the bunker at *10 Cloverfield Lane* (USA 2016), somewhere in Louisiana, the main character frees herself from the perverse bondage of the insane doomer, but in doing so must also give up the temporary protection of his bunker. She gets into the car in a hazmat suit made from a shower curtain, turns on the radio, and hears the motivational announcement from Houston on an old AM radio channel: "If you are hearing this and aren't in a safe zone, head north to Baton Rouge. But if you have any medical training or combat experience, we need help. There are people in Houston. There are survivors at Mercy Hospital. Please help" (M97) – and that's exactly what she does. In *A Quiet Place: Part II,* the radio even becomes the means of choice to beat back the aliens with their extremely noise-sensitive hearing organs by a blaring sound. So without a radio, you're always in a bad situation, in modern as well as postmodern times.

Restarting radio broadcasts as a glimmer of hope – organization of reconstruction

Also in *Y – The Last Man* (USA 2021), where all male mammals worldwide have perished within a day, hope briefly arises in the midst of the powerless world, as Dolly Parton's voice sounds for a few seconds on the silenced radio – until the static starts again and despair returns (S01E03M44). In this world, where electricity is only available if you have a solar panel for your own use, but everything has long since fallen into disrepair, nuclear power plants are threatening to explode due to a lack of (mostly male) engineers. Phone calls here are only possible by satellite phone, otherwise the rest of the population is largely cut off from the information supply – conspiracy theories are spreading. When the radios go silent, the blackout has probably long since become the new normal. Nevertheless, these fictions cannot do without the image of the great shutdown itself: all the warning signs described can be suppressed if you're not directly affected by them – but seeing the blackout with your own eyes invariably signals to the characters that the rules of the game are now being rewritten. *Fear the Walking Dead* tells the prequel to the zombie apocalypse in its first season. At the beginning of the third episode, all the early warning signals have already been worked through: the radio is full of horror news, the phones no longer work, chaos reigns on the streets, the stores are empty, some even already have a physical confrontation with a biting undead – but the characters still do not really want to believe it against better judgment. Even when passing a hospital under fire, they don't really understand what is going

10th stage: Only the image of modernity shutting down itself confirms impending doom

to happen, and one must never underestimate the power of repression. The awareness of the end of the world is only sealed by the view from the Hollywood Hills, from where one can see all the way to downtown Los Angeles. While we are looking into the horrified faces of the survivors, the reflection of the car windows in this all-important scene shows how, like a game of dominoes, all the blocks of the city shut down one after the other until only the fires are visible. Although the general mood had already been stricken before, it is now that the people really know what fear means.

The best view of the blackout is, of course, from higher up, such as in the small web series *Fear the Walking Dead: Flight 462* (USA 2015–2016). Shortly after the outbreak of the devastating pandemic, one of the last planes takes off before the airspace is sealed off. A boy watches from the window as the lights go out below him (cf. fig. 18) – but everyone is distracted by the first case of infection, which is raging in the washroom despite the landing approach. The fate of the aircraft is sealed when the pilot announces that the power has failed in the entire area of the approached city and that they will return to Los Angeles. But they won't get there, because they're on the very plane that Nick watches in the sky from the ground in the third episode of *Fear the Walking Dead:* judging by the style of flight, the pilot seems to have already made contact with the otherworldly.

> Standard motif: view from above of the cities shutting down

When the global extent of the blackout catastrophe is to be made unmistakably clear, the camera switches to an impossible 'bird's eye view' (better:

> Image of the cooled darkened planet from space

satellite perspective) and shows the electrically illuminated globe as it gradually shuts down, as if a
black wave were laying over the world, for example
right at the beginning of the pilot episode of *Revolution* (USA 2012–2014, S01E01M03). Here, from
one moment to the next, all electronics on the
planet have become useless: "Everything stopped
working. We weren't prepared." (S01E01M04)
Thus the fate of modernity is sealed.

At the end of all the harbingers is the image of
a cooled, deactivated Earth, with which the transition to post-modernity is completed. This is remarkable because the characters in these fictional worlds
can only indirectly form an idea of the extent of the
catastrophe. While the viewers of such films and
series can comprehensively trace and understand
the downfall through the perspectives of the various
storylines, the actors in fiction are dependent on
their individual slices of reality: looking out the
window is not enough to know whether it is just a
regional power outage or a serious blackout, because after a few hours everything can be back to
normal even in the case of a power failure, and it is
difficult to say what the situation is like in the rest
of the world without functioning communication.
Only on the basis of the advance warnings described
above is it possible to assess whether the blackout is
local and temporary – or a serious matter. Then, as
soon as it is uncertain whether the power will come
back at all, the ambiguity begins as to whether modernity will continue.

Figures perceive
only a limited
section of reality –
severity of the
crisis cannot be
readily assessed

Figure 18: There's a tense mood on the plane of Fear the Walking Dead – Flight 462, *because there's "this flu that's going around" in the air. Just before the plane is scheduled to land, a young boy watches as the city below them gradually shuts down (S01E07). As the blackout spreads across the country, there is no place left to land.*

Because the characters, just like people in reality, can hardly assess whether the problem will quickly pass or manifest itself during a power outage, the warning signs described in this chapter are so important for them: the indicators are the only way to tell with any degree of certainty what you're dealing with in advance of and during a power outage. "People don't know what's coming" (S01E04M02), explains a reporter in the Russian blackout series *Avanpost,* which is the source of the great uncertainty and fear that drives the characters in the films and series not always to their best deeds. However, anyone who recognizes the signals in

Only power failure or devastating blackout? Warning signs of the escalation levels enable differentiation and appropriate behavior

good time and makes preparations, who doesn't wait until the big chaos to do their last shopping, who takes the obvious clues seriously, who gets a radio and switches it on, and who follows the instructions of the authorities, still has the best cards – at least that's what the fictional blackout scenarios tell us – when the end of the modern world threatens. Fortunately, beyond the dramatizing and exaggerated scenarios of film and television entertainment, we can rely on the fact that modernity will remain with us for quite a while yet – but it does no harm to the characters, like oneself, to make one's preparations for a crisis in the awareness that all that we have become accustomed to in an electrified world cannot be taken for granted. In film and television, at least, people are in danger of breaking psychologically from the fact that their world does not seem to be made for eternity.

6. THE PSYCHOLOGY OF THE BLACKOUT: HOW CHARACTERS REACT TO THE CRISIS

Precisely because life in the modern age hardly knows any exceptional situations, supply shortages occur very rarely and power outages never last for long, a blackout potentially represents a considerable psychological burden for people in reality as well as for the characters in films and television, and not everyone can cope with it well. The TAB study mentioned in chapter 2 already concludes: "A prolonged power blackout will create uncertainty and fear among the population, and also create threats to life and limb. According to the research on the behaviour of individuals and groups in disaster situations, it can be expected that even a power blackout would give rise both to antisocial, illegal and aggressive conduct and also to empathy, a willingness to help and rational and decisive action." (Petermann et al. 2011, 39) However, how people would really behave in such an emergency situation without a historical example remains unclear, and it is difficult to make generalizable statements about how people would actually deal with exceeding their psychological resilience limits.

Blackout films and television series often devote special attention to these psychological consequences of such an event. Narratives that focus on the social tensions and individual experiences of loss of control and fear of the future that accompany a

> Blackout chamber plays and ensemble films illuminate psychological consequences of (impending) catastrophe

blackout are often ensemble pieces with a manageable number of characters whose souls are illuminated in greater detail, as well as chamber-play-like scenarios that place their characters in a clearly delineated cosmos of action with specific rules within which they must prove themselves – because there is no saving 'outside' to which one could take refuge.

The Wolf Hour (USA 2019) represents a perfect example in this regard – even though (or precisely because?) the film spends 81 minutes building toward the blackout. Set in 1977, the atmospheric psychological thriller closes in on its main character June (Naomi Watts) in a cluttered stuffy apartment in the middle of the Bronx, a New York City neighborhood known for the poverty that prevails there. June was once a well-respected author, known for her provocations against the patriarchal establishment, but has now been cooped up in her late grandmother's small apartment for quite some time. Plagued by anxiety disorders, it seems impossible for her to leave her home. The garbage bags pile up, she has all groceries delivered to her doorstep, and with her last ounce of strength she calls a "midnight cowboy" – the main thing is that she doesn't have to go out the door. There are terrible dangers outside: the gangs that make the sidewalks unsafe, the constant ringing at the intercom, where no one answers, and even the policeman (who shows up only a week after the emergency call about the stalking) only wants to help in exchange for sexual favors: "this place, this country, is changing. Not for the

The Wolf Hour: New York slums facing historic blackout in 1977 before social collapse

best" – with which he speaks mainly of himself (M54). On the radio and television there are constant reports of a serial killer who preys on women with long brown hair – June sees herself as the ideal victim according to the prey pattern. And then there is this glowing heat, hardly bearable... Not without reason her best friend calls the residential area a "time bomb" (M30), the paid acquaintance means, it is "a war zone" (M65), and even the murderer signs his 'business cards' with a "Hello from the gutters of New York" (M20). If June didn't have her two lamps shining in the evening, one could think that the blackout had already begun here, at least life in this fictional dark world is a single torment.

When she gradually runs out of the advance for her second book, which she has been writing for four years, she has to admit to herself that she can't go on like this. She whips out the typewriter and types so fast and furiously that she doesn't even hear the constant ringing terror anymore. But to get the finished book to the publisher, she would have to get out of the house. So she hires her delivery boy to help out as a courier – but the manuscript, of which there is no copy, doesn't seem to have arrived at its destination, and so neither does her check. Her misery is perfect when then, after a lightning strike, the city's ailing and overloaded power grid collapses. While the omnipresent hum of the air conditioners falls silent, a mixture of shouting and sirens now dominates, occasionally a helicopter with a glaring spotlight roars over the rooftops. Just as in the real New York City on July 13, 1977 (cf. chapter

During blackout, violence and anarchy outside doors exacerbate psychotic fear of leaving home

2), the looting is not long in coming, there are shootings, parts of the city are in flames – but the authorities, the radio assures, have everything under control: "Keep cool, stay calm." (M87, cf. fig. 19) The danger, previously kept at a distance with more or less success, moves ever closer to June, because the police are even more overstretched than usual, and the first rioters have already gained access to the apartment building. She tries to barricade herself in – but it is too late. Finally, she watches from the window as an African-American, a supposed looter, is beaten up by a police officer, and she thinks she sees her delivery boy with her badly needed money. When she manages to overcome her fear and leaves the apartment (only to discover that it is not the young man with her fee from the publisher at all) she sees the sunrise over the dark blazing city. It is like a rebirth for her: she has been able to fight her anxiety in this *Wolf Hour* (German title: "Hour of Fear"). Her new book is called, of course, "Season in the Abyss" (M93).

The Wolf Hour succeeds in drawing a psychological portrait of a blackout without needing much blackout, because in this New York modernity seems to be at an end anyway – even when the electricity flows it is as if it were not there. People sweat, are constantly on edge, get irritated by every little thing and at the same time provoke themselves at every opportunity. Sometimes they shoot each other for an ice cream cone. The film produces a restlessness that is transmitted from the air of June's apartment to the viewer. That's about what life should

Cinematic atmosphere of terror corresponds to experiences of uncertainty during a blackout

feel like during the blackout: like sitting on a powder keg whose fuse has already been lit. All the candles here do not convey a feeling of coziness, but of
a sacrificial ritual to which June must surrender (cf.
fig. 19). Even though the angst-ridden June may be
the "ghetto lunatic" (M46), in the midst of this
bleak atmosphere, it is all too easy to empathize
with her mind of dread at the sight of her. The
blackout, with the defenselessness it unleashes, produces an atmosphere of high tension in which there
can be little trust, hope, or closeness.

*Figure 19: After months of living in self-imposed isolation, anxious best-selling
author June Leigh (Naomi Watts) leaves her apartment during* The Wolf Hour
*(M86) of the Great Blackout of 1977 in New York City. Only gazing into the
sunrise against the backdrop of the dark city will give her the strength to return
to normality.*

A similarly electrified mood prevails in *The
Trigger Effect* (USA 1996), whereby the film title is
to be understood literally: the city-wide blackout
triggers an escalation of the already tense basic

The Trigger Effect:
General social high
voltage escalates
due to blackout

mood in the city. Again, this time in Los Angeles, people suffer from intense heat and sultriness. Exhausted young married couple Matthew ('*Twin Peaks* agent' Kyle MacLachlan) and Annie have left their tiny daughter with a nanny to rest from the never-ending house renovation and the little tormentor constantly suffering from fever. Listlessness and cynicism spread through the young couple – the date is supposed to remedy the situation. But the movie night turns out to be less pleasurable than hoped: the people in the mall are all so irritable that it only takes a small occasion for the anger to ignite. Where the discontent in the consumer temple comes from remains unclear, but every jostle, every remark, every look sets people on edge. The mood in the cinema is also tense, because the husband is too cowardly to say anything when his wife is insulted – the social peace is hanging by a thread that is about to snap. When the film projector shuts down for a few seconds, the big blackout announces itself, which then haunts the city a day later at night and brings the barrel to overflow.

The great collective rage does not diminish when the problems become visible and palpable the next day. The feverish little daughter needs her antibiotic, but because the phones don't work, the doctor can't call the pharmacy, and the pharmacist can't access the prescriptions because the computer isn't working. The grim-faced guy at the pharmacy doesn't show much cooperation in this particular emergency situation, however, as he simply admits to the hopeless Matthew, "I don't like you." (M20)

Blackout increases general irritability and reduces mutual trust

Even at the hospital, the unnerved father cannot be helped because the emergency generator has failed. He feels compelled (and also somehow invigorated by the risk) to steal the medicine – in the face of this small danger, even lust returns for a brief moment. But by then Annie's old good buddy Joe is already knocking on the door. Because the radio doesn't broadcast on any channel and the TV won't turn on without power, the two of them pounce on the rumors the carpenter has to offer: core meltdown, meteorite impact, one just doesn't know – but the one about shootings and dead people sounds plausible, because "everyone is freaking out" (M28). Because no other information is available, the trio forms their own opinion and feels confirmed that the city is going downhill: there are fistfights, traffic jams and sirens everywhere. As long as the danger is calculable, Annie even seems to find a certain pleasure in the whole chaos. The men, on the other hand, want to arm themselves, but the price of shotguns has tripled in the meantime, and they can only pay with valuables at a unserious estimate. In the night, someone breaks into the house, the neighbor shoots the thief, although he holds only a knife in the hand (see fig. 20). The neighborhood plans to barricade the residential area with roadblocks and debates about the confiscation of a neighbor's electric generator. Now everything seems possible, because people here now only think about themselves.

Figure 20: In The Trigger Effect *(M46), nerves are on edge. Thugs roam the suburbs, getting shot in the back by the neighborhood. During the blackout, the law still exists, but different rules apply – with fatal consequences.*

It is therefore not surprising that the protagonists of *The Trigger Effect* try to flee the city and avoid the potentially dangerous fellow citizens in the countryside (even if they themselves are not always exactly harmless). Cynically, this very plan puts them in danger. When they stop on a country road next to an apparently abandoned car to steal fuel, they get into an armed confrontation with the gangster who had apparently stolen the abandoned vehicle earlier. The sinister criminal shoots Joe when he is denied a ride and takes the car. No one wants to stop for the little family in danger – they could be wolves in sheep's clothing, after all. With that, people have finally turned into the snarling wolves that give a taste of what to expect in the first

Disputes quickly turn to violence in both urban and rural areas – but trust and solidarity are rewarded

scene of the film: the blackout brings out 'the bad' in people who only think of themselves. And yet there are moments of unexpected goodness: when Matthew tries to get a car to drive his shot buddy to the hospital, he encounters a rural resident who is not particularly helpful at first, because no one trusts anyone anymore. Again, guns are pointed at each other – and again, it only takes one spark to make the situation explode. Only when Matthew – in the sight of the resident's innocent little daughter – finally puts down the shotgun, the other decides to help his fellow citizen in obvious need and drives him to the police. And the couple (always arguing at the beginning of the film) also seems to have grown together again by overcoming the danger, because it proves that in everyday life as in a state of emergency only the community is resilient, while the lonely always have the worse card.

The flight from the city into the seemingly pro-tective rusticity is a recurring motif that is used again and again in blackout fictions as well as in the disaster genre in general, but regularly leads to dis-aster. In *Radioflash* (USA 2019), in keeping with the title, a global electromagnetic pulse (EMP) occurs for unclear reasons: the entire power supply in North America has collapsed. The smart Reese, who has obsessively acquired amazing problem-solving skills in immersive computer games (while at the same time fantasizing about a controllable parallel world), manages with the help of a car battery to put the old amateur radio into operation to contact her grandfather, who is excellently prepared for the

Radioflash: Different hazard perceptions lead to different handling strategies (displacement and actionism)

'end of the world'. She should come with her father to his place in the country as soon as possible – he has everything you need to survive. Daddy, on the other hand, sleeps in on the day of the apocalypse and wants to make himself a cup of coffee in peace and quiet – although, of course, there is no more water coming out of the tap. The strange grandfather figure, on the other hand, sitting on a huge stockpile of supplies and in front of a dozen old radios, warns via walkie talkie that the EMP has practically wiped out civilization. Grandpa knows it's about to get uncomfortable in the cities ("The clock is ticking", M25) – but the drive to his place turns into a gauntlet: on the unlit streets with hectic and overtired drivers, accidents happen again and again, cars break down and become dangerous obstacles. During a blackout, it is advisable to make journeys only in an emergency and to travel at an appropriate speed. In any case, the inevitable crash occurs and the father suffers severe internal bleeding. Just before he dies, a bearded old man figure appears to the daughter in her imagination. Reese fears it, because it already announced the death of her cancer-stricken mother. Now he appears as the prophet of the decay of her accustomed modern life, as the grim reaper of modernity itself.

Gradually it becomes apparent that escaping to the countryside does not come free of charge. When a helpful farmer wants to drive the orphan to Grandpa, the ominous old ghost appears again and prophesies something bad: the oh-so-sympathetic young man, whose car has supposedly broken down

Escape to the supposedly peaceful countryside leads into a world of loneliness

on the side of the road, only wants to rob the farmer's truck – no matter what the cost. As the good-natured farmer had foreseen, a "real back-woods territory" full of "trappers, old gold seekers, even some outlaws" is waiting behind the mountains (M46). Even if these cliché characters are only alle-gories for the stereotypical fears and insinuations of the townspeople, they point to the impossibility of simply escaping the blackout with its consequences. Thus, in the vastness of nothingness, Reese comes across a peculiar clan of three who live off a junk-yard and bear hunting: a neglected man dressed in bear cases rescues them from the killer and takes them to his creepy mother in a mechanical wheel-chair, who feeds them bear meat. Bears play a big role here in general. These strange recluses care mostly about their own well-being and don't give a damn about humans. Here in the (even before the blackout) practically lawless territory, the news of the blackout in the cities hasn't even hit home yet: "Well, see, that's why we live in the woods. Power ain't a problem for people out here," says the witch-like woman (M66). In exchange, the people seem to have a problem with her social skills, because when Reese tries to escape from the three psychos, she is imprisoned: obviously, the horror granny has some plans for her unexpected female guest, there are just too few mating opportunities for her two lonely bachelors. Her son and his boy Quinn, she concocts, should not remain single forever – so the young woman comes as called to maintain the pre-modern microcosm.

The three cast-offs, who live primarily off the garbage of modern industrial society, are stuck in an archaic pre-modern way of life that is even more anti-modern than the post-modern life during the blackout. The curious episode on the eerie property serves as an exaggerated portrayal of a degenerate society that makes a living out a desolate existence in a scrapped modernity that is empty of electricity. Because they know no other way, the pre-modern characters do not recognize the absurdity of their existence, from which only modernization could help: rationalization, urbanization, electrification. The initial appeal of the naïve idea that one could sit comfortably on the porch and drink tea "while the world beyond them trees is burning" (M76) is quickly lost, because even the seemingly self-sufficient people from the countryside, who do not want to do without industrial goods, are dependent on a functioning modernity in the city. Here in the middle of nowhere, there are not even the memories of a modern life, but the young woman from the city is still visibly attached to what she had: the tablet computer with the last percent of battery becomes the elixir of life for her, because the memories of carefree modern times can be found on it. They are the shadows of moments of shared happiness with mother and father, taking place against a modern backdrop. The awareness that a modern life has recently existed gives her the strength to break out of the haunted house together with Quinn (who is also being held against his will), to kill his brutal father – and thus to finally get rid of the ghostly figure who

Hillbilly life stands for regression to pre-modern mistakes – what cannot be accepted if one knew modernity

reminds her of the painful experiences of the transition to the new post-modern life. Reese doesn't need her anymore, because when she is finally safe with her grandfather, she makes her peace with post-modernity.

Together with Grandpa and Quinn, who has escaped from the nightmare house, Reese begins a new life in Grandpa's forest cabin, which is crammed with useful things from past modern times that will no longer 'grow' without electricity and thus without industrial production. While Reese comes to terms with the new life in the post-modern age and learns to survive with simple means in harmony with nature, Quinn, on the other hand, shows enthusiasm for the remnants of the technological age: on the tablet, which has been recharged by a generator, all the text messages that could not be transmitted since the beginning of the blackout suddenly start coming in – apparently the Internet and cell phone service are working again. Was the whole horrible nightmare perhaps just an all-too-realistic computer game, like the one Reese had encountered at the beginning of the film? Or could modernity be resuscitated at the last moment? And will it be possible to domesticate it again after all the experiences of horror?

Hope for the return of modernity makes post-modern existence easier to endure

This uncertainty also plagues the characters in *Then There Was* (USA 2014), an aesthetically and narratively remarkable blackout drama that has received little attention from critics and box office. The film looks into the lives of the inhabitants of a

Then There Was: Many psychological mechanisms to cope with blackout – but only together they have a chance

small US town that is caught off guard by a nation-wide blackout and has to come to terms with the new situation. The comparatively detailed characters develop different psychological strategies for dealing with the crisis, which only gradually emerges as a national catastrophe. A widowed former military doctor has retreated to his house with respectable supplies, shotgun and video recordings of his deceased wife, and spends his lonely days playing chess against anonymous acquaintances he finds via amateur radio – but the power outage deprives him of even this last virtual company. The dedicated and socially respected local sheriff, on the other hand, imagines that he alone can ensure law and order despite the increasing unrest, while food reserves are gradually drying up. The experienced military man warns of the countless refugees from the cities who will soon overrun the villages in the hope of finding shelter and food: "Take a look outside. Can't you feel it? It's already begun." (M30) While radio and television are off the air, he seems to be able to offer the only trustworthy information, so the villagers follow his advice and prepare for the onslaught with barricaded windows and loaded guns. However, the young couple, who has to cope with a miscarriage in the midst of all the madness, can best survive the crisis together, as the lovers give each other moral support. For instance, when the supplies run low, the caring husband prepares a candlelight dinner for his wife: there are only a few beans, pasta and crackers on the plates, but who says you can't imagine sitting in a romantic French

restaurant with specialties from Normandy and a
good bottle of wine? As long as the two are together,
the film tells us, any crisis can be weathered:
"You're all I have." (M64) Even the strike against an
assassinating group of escaped convicts can only be
waged as a group – alone, each individual, even with
appropriate skills and a high capacity for suffering,
is defenseless against the dangers of a blackout.

While the people in the village are gradually beginning to feel the extent of the crisis, a group of
young people who set out on a longer hiking trip are
taken off guard by the crisis when they return from
their adventure. Just a moment ago, they were
dreaming lightheartedly over a bottle of champagne
about their grand plans for how they would like to
settle into modern society: in five years, they want to
be in the Olympics and married, they want to have a
publicly traded start-up and win their first election in
Washington. Then, when they return from the
wilderness a few days later, the car is gone, the cell
phones unexpectedly don't work, and the neglected
streets are full of trash and bloodstains. While the
other characters have had time to gradually get used
to the social degeneration, the young people have to
come to terms with the new situation from one
moment to the next – and as members of Generation
Z, they are at the same time probably the most
unprepared for the dawn of post-modernity,
although they will potentially still have to spend the
longest of their lives under these conditions (see
chapter 8). Because they find only rotten frozen
goods and dead bodies in most abandoned houses,

Getting used to the
consequences of
the blackout takes
time – young
people are hardly
psychologically
equipped for post-
modern life

they can hardly believe their luck when they track down a house full of canned goods in the attic of the retired military doctor. They finally meet the group of escaped convicts who, due to their pathological lack of empathy, cynically cope best psychologically with the situation: the anarchic conditions are a playground for the rapists and murderers, whose rules they know best – for there are none left (cf. fig. 21).

The longer the blackout lasts, the greater the despair of each individual, because with each passing day the uncertainty grows as to whether the power will return in time or whether modernity will have been disfigured beyond recognition by then, so that even turning it back on would not change the decay of the world. The high level of nervousness and the collective loss of confidence lead again and again to avoidable confrontations up to armed violence. When the lights suddenly come back on at night and the full extent of the accumulated horrors becomes visible, the impression is created that even after the electricity returns, it will not be possible to restore normal modern conditions. In the streets, the lights are on again, the refrigerators hum as always, and in the house of the widower shot by the brutal felons, the TV turns on again with his wife's cassette: "There's a good world out there. ... Don't give up on the world," she had left her husband as a last message (M89). However, there is much more of a feeling that the modern world has long since taken its leave: even if electricity returns, the experiences of the anti-modern will overshadow the new life and will not be equally digestible by everyone.

Psychological consequences grow with each day without electricity, because it remains uncertain whether return to modernity (even with electricity) will still be possible

Figure 21: In Then There Was *(M41), tension is high in a small U.S. town as supplies begin to dry up after a week-long blackout. Escaped dangerous criminals shoot indiscriminately to capture a few canned goods and bottles of water. In their hopelessness, some citizens even join the organized rapists.*

The two sisters Nell and Eva from *Into the Forest* (CA 2015), on the other hand, have resigned themselves to the end of modernity at the end of the film and no longer expect to return. At the beginning of the blackout, the two young women live with their caring father in a neat forest villa. Unfortunately, the roof isn't quite leak-proof, so the rain comes through, and since there will soon be no division of labor and thus no craftsmen, this could become a problem later. Actually, the family of three could sit out the threatening collapse of the nationwide power supply here quite well, but there is a lack of gasoline for the generator and the converter for the small solar cell has not yet been delivered. Small mistakes are now taking revenge: Nell, who wants to study medicine, left the trunk open at night

Remembrance of past community and earlier modern life can make blackout easier to bear

when she took a flashlight out of the car at the beginning of the nationwide blackout – the next morning the car won't start, the battery is dead. The replacement accumulator is also without power and
the three are stuck in their cabin. After ten days
without power, when the radio already only sends
static, the father has a creative but disastrous idea:
he starts the car with the help of the motor of a converted chainsaw, but when he later wants to use it
again to cut down a tree, a nut that has not been
tightened enough comes loose and the chain flies
off. The father bleeds to death, the daughters are
left grieving alone, and Nell suffers terribly from the
fact that her negligence with the trunk door seems
to have set off a devastating chain of coincidences.
While Eva tries to distract herself with excessive bal-
let training (without music, only to the metronome),
Nell falls into depression – only studying for the en-
trance exam, which will probably never happen,
gives her some support. With only rice and beans
left, every memory of carefree modern times now
becomes a sanctuary: the last pieces of gum, a piece
of chocolate, and, of course, the video recordings of
happy days with Mom and Dad before a serious illness separated them. After months of disciplined ab-
stention, they sacrifice part of their scarce gasoline
reserves in order to revive the memories of modern
times and the lost community for a few minutes
with the help of the videotape (cf. fig. 22).

Figure 22: With mold eating away at their home and no help in sight, the fully orphaned sisters of Into the Forest *(M57) imagine for one last moment what life was like in modern times: the television grants a vivid glimpse of past community that will never return. The two decide to come to terms with post-modernity, but will they survive the threatening loneliness?*

But the momentary distraction cannot protect them from the gradual intrusion of post-modernity into their previously protected cosmos. After some time, Nell's boyfriend shows up and tells of the circulating conspiracy theories about how the blackout might have occurred, and of the psychologically disintegrated city people who continue to go to the mailbox every morning even though there is no more letters – "like a dissociative fugue" (M43), a mental illness, Nell explains, in which the memory of one's past is erased. The two young women, on the other hand, gradually lose their memory of modern life when there are no more canned goods,

Maintaining familiar routines and protecting family bonds as a coping mechanism the first maggots crawl in the rice, and Eva is raped by a stranger. With the experience of social decay, the hope of a return to modern conditions also dies. Nell's boyfriend briefly awakens in the girl the spirit of adventure and desire to move with him to the East, where there is supposedly electricity again, but at the last moment she turns away from the dream and returns to her sister in the parental home and thus to post-modern reality.

When Eva realizes she is pregnant from the rape, the two young women must adjust to raising the child alone and without modern tools. Nell has another reason to take up her self-study of medicine, and they learn to distinguish edible from poisonous forest plants, pickle meat in salt, and make soap. But the house is increasingly eaten up by the encroaching rain, the wood is rotten, and mold is spreading. When the ceiling literally threatens to fall on Nell and Eva's heads and the house becomes uninhabitable, Eva wants to burn the villa down: humans have existed for hundreds of thousands of years, electricity only since 140, and as long as they have each other, they could do without the decomposed house. They take only a few blankets, books and mementos from the house and retreat into a tree stump. When the house goes up in flames, the memory of modernity is finally overcome, which the two experience at that moment as a liberation, because with the nostalgia for times past also disappears the unfounded longing that the lost modernity could be brought back. Whether the two will sur-

Detachment from nostalgic memories of modernity necessary to survive in post-modernity

vive the challenge of a life under the open sky remains uncertain at the end of the film, despite a hopeful undertone, but at least they have finally made their peace with the end of modern life.

The mentally disturbed prepper Howard, who lives at *10 Cloverfield Lane* (USA 2016), on the other hand, wants to hold on to his naïve and pathological idea of a modern bourgeois life by any means necessary. Longingly awaiting the end of the world, he has built a shelter in his backyard that imitates *Home, Sweet Home* under the protective earth. When heavy flashes and multiplying power outages announce an attack, he races to his bunker. On his way home, he (accidentally?) rams a car and he takes the injured Michelle into his domicile. She wakes up in the shelter and has not noticed the takeover of the aliens and the global blackout. She is sure that she has been abducted by Howard, but is informed about the situation by Emmett, who is also in the bunker: the young man was hired by the corpulent prepper as a helper in the construction of the bunker and has known Howard for years. He has "a black belt in conspiracy theories," the simple young man says of the amateur bunker builder, who is afraid of everything: "El Kaisa, Russia, South Korea..." – "You mean North Korea." – "Is that the crazy one?" (M30) In the meantime, the prepper even talks about Martians who might have finally made it here – with which he disqualifies himself completely.

Blackout provokes emergence of conspiracy theories to which the lonely are particularly susceptible

In any case, the three of them have electricity in the disturbingly cozy substitute home, even if it fluctuates occasionally. In general, the prepper has created a self-sufficient system, with air filters and water supply, in which he can stage an almost normal modern life complete with stove, toilet and entertainment electronics. After Howard confesses the accident and Michelle is assured of the real danger beyond the thick steel door, the three lead an all in all peaceful life, though Howard is occasionally prone to outbursts of rage and is jealous of young Emmett. Despite the occasional wrath of the man of the house, the two young people are happy not to have to wander around in the powerless world contaminated by the aliens. Together they pass the time with board games, nostalgic evergreens from the jukebox and ice cream. Although modernity has long been eliminated above them, they pretend that it is still progressing, but they only become aware of this self-deception when they sometimes remember the 'good old days' – the dream of designing one's own fashion or becoming a professional track and field athlete. Howard's dream, on the other hand, has come true: "Everything I wanted to do, I did: I focused on being prepared. And I was. And here we are." (M36) There is something religious about a life lived in hope of the apocalypse, but the one-time satellite technician lacks attachment to an overarching mythological or spiritual order, leaving his faith empty and unfulfilled – an obsessive neurosis without value in itself (cf. fig. 23).

Preppers live in pseudo-religious hope for the fulfillment of their own apocalyptic prophecy – and yet remain lonely

Figure 23: Beneath the ground of the estate of 10 Cloverfield Lane *(M33), it looks at first glance as if life could simply go on as before after the alien blackout. In fact, social peace in this distressed group is built only on lies, unequal power relations, and the ability to suffer. Even if this life seems modern at first glance, it is the exact opposite.*

However, it becomes clear that the frightened man is not really the 'concerned fellow citizen' and the good-natured father figure he pretends to be when Michelle accidentally finds traces of a girl who has been missing for years in the bunker. Apparently she's not the first child surrogate the perverted prepper has dragged into his bunker, because since his biological daughter moved away to live with his ex-wife, he apparently no longer has anyone. Because with the end of modernity, the already crushing loneliness only becomes more intense: in the dreariness of the bunker, being alone becomes a burden that not everyone can cope with. First the girl and now Michelle apparently have to take the rap for the fact that the maniac has someone to take care of in his illusory modernity, even if no one has

Longing for an eternal modernity that withstands all dangers is childishly naive and unfulfillable

189

asked for his 'help'. "People are strange creatures. You can't always convince them that safety is in their own best interest." (M49) The pathological misconception is that modern life of course always involves calculated risks, and that protecting against every conceivable life risk leads to oppression and stagnation – working against modernization. Howard longs for an everlasting modernity that continues to run for him even when no one wants to inhabit it with him, even when it is already at an end.

Michelle, on the other hand, can't and won't hold out like a rat in the sewers – what would come after that, even if she survived the year or two underground? She finally gets rid of the bunker fetishist (who in the meantime also has his construction helper on his conscience, dissolved in a foresightedly stored acid barrel), frees herself from the facility and leads a fierce fight against the new 'neighbors', the alien guests, which she finishes off with an impromptu Molotov cocktail. When, battle-hardened and thus self-confident, she finally hears the voices of other people on the car radio again, she decides to join the resistance against the uninvited visitors. Maybe modernity can be saved after all.

> It is not the fearful preppers who save the world, but the brave ones who want to live in a real modernity

But life without protection in a deelectrified world is no bed of roses. The main character Zac in the curious New Zealand science fiction classic *The Quiet Earth* (NZ 1985) had to experience this firsthand. When he wakes up after a failed suicide attempt, all the people seem to have disappeared off the face of the Earth. Obviously, something went wrong with the experiment to equip the world with

> Loneliness after blackout leads to despair – only the presence of other people can protect against it

an all-encompassing power grid. Now Zac is probably the last person on the planet. The film becomes a psychogram of total loneliness – from denial and anger, depression and excess to despair and eventual acceptance of the new life. As long as the electricity still flows and he can make his hopeful radio announcements, television and music keep him a little company, and he can settle into a brightly lit castle, this state can be endured for a while, despite all the agonies. But when, after five days, the electricity is also gone (because there is no one left to maintain and control the power grid), total mental derangement sets in: first he thinks he is God, then he finally wants to shoot himself. Only the contact with two other survivors gives him the courage to go on living, even if everything becomes more complicated with electricity via generator. At the same time the three feel that they are dependent on each other in an empty world without power, they dance to piano music and make the best of their hopeless situation. If it weren't for Zac's guilt of having caused the devastating effect, including the blackout, himself. Only the destruction of the "net", which seems to be responsible for the disappearance of the people, could end the mysterious effect and thus also the blackout, but after the explosion Zac ends up not in the afterlife, but in an even stranger parallel universe... The de-electrified post-modernity is obviously not so easy to escape.

In *Fin* (*The End*, S 2012), the conditions are also confusing and psychologically challenging. Some former best friends meet for a big reunion in a country house – only Ángel, called "the Prophet" by everyone, has not appeared. Under the influence of a drug cocktail, he had said crazy things about an impending 'end of the world' at their last encounter 20 years ago and ended up in a psychiatric ward. On this evening, the time has come: the sky is brightly lit for a moment, and after a second, not a single technical device is working anymore. Even though the special effect suggests that an astronomical event such as a supernova including a gamma flash could be responsible for the global blackout, the cause of the blackout is actually relatively unimportant for the individuals – what is decisive are the consequences that those affected have to deal with. Nevertheless, the characters agonize over the ignorance in which they were left after the blackout. In the post-electrified age in which the aged clique has landed, nothing is granted, not even the time: the modern world has simply stopped.

> Blackout creates lack of information and dangerous ignorance that produces uncertainty

They could actually sit it out together for now, but overnight someone from the group disappears and the necessary search for the missing person becomes an opportunity to also look for answers. But on the way through the mountains to the next larger village, the group gradually disintegrates: one by one, they disappear without a trace. Anyone who separates from the community for too long or decides to set out on their own is simply gone, as if vanished into thin air. Obviously, it is not a wise

> Whoever breaks away from the community in the crisis is lost – 'last men' survive only with each other

idea to try to go it alone during such a situation. People become restless because everything is unclear and thus the future is also uncertain. The urge for security and orientation becomes insatiable. Every time they reach a house, a restaurant, any place of refuge, the first thought is of the telephone, which of course remains silent. Only the wreckage of the airplane (cf. fig. 24) testifies to the fact that they share a fate with all of humanity: the disturbing drawings of doom that Ángel had prophetically made before his death gradually come true – until in the end only two figures remain. As they drift out to sea on a boat under a starry sky, they realize that they will only survive this crisis if they stay together: "Maybe of [the stars] we see, none is left. Perhaps we see the light of stars that have long since gone out. Perhaps the same thing is happening to us. Maybe we merely exist as long as others are watching us." (M85; own translation) They may be the last people in the switched-off world – but as long as they just stay together, they may be able to find this life worth living even without electricity.

The psychological methods of the characters in the blackout scenarios to deal with the unexpected or hoped-for demise of the modern way of life are diverse, and yet commonalities and recurring constellations can be identified. Because hardly any of the protagonists expected such a devastating event, there are hardly any appropriate handling strategies to deal with the catastrophe in a meaningful way: feelings of powerlessness and cognitive overload develop. The harder and faster the consequences of

Blackout creates powerlessness – minimum amount of crisis preparedness increases resilience

the blackout strike, the greater the psychological effects: if an end to the blackout is uncertain or if the consequences are no longer manageable for the individual, feelings of insecurity and anxiety threaten to escalate and overwhelm the hopeless. Only those characters who have displayed a minimum degree of crisis awareness even before the blackout occurs are able to react to the new situation as appropriately as possible if the worst comes to the worst. They are still most likely to come to terms with the unfamiliar situation.

Figure 24: For a long time, the distraught characters of Fin (M70) cherish the hope that the blackout only had a regional impact. Gradually, however, they discover abandoned villages, wrecked airplanes and have to understand that they may be the last people on Earth.

Excessive crisis preparedness, on the other hand, is usually not an expression of special psychological resilience against a catastrophic event, but rather testifies to a naïve longing for orderly surroundings that cannot be maintained indefinitely

Overcautious and lone fighters have little chance of survival (even with unlimited resources) under conditions of a widespread and prolonged crisis such as a blackout, even in the protected special space of the private sphere. The impending demise of modernity hits these figures particularly hard when, against all expectations, they cannot maintain their accustomed lives despite all preparations. The idea of mastering the transition to post-modernity as a lone fighter is usually punished. In the blackout fictions in film and television, the best chances of surviving the blackout as unscathed as possible are those who join forces with others and support each other morally and practically in life, and who are prepared not to suppress the new situation but to acknowledge the changed reality of life and act responsibly under its more difficult conditions. Memories from modern times can facilitate the transition to the new normality of the blackout as well as the speedy return to familiar circumstances – otherwise there is a threat of nihilistic experiences of loneliness that make it impossible to survive the crisis psychologically.

7. TERROR WAITS IN THE DARK: BLACKOUTS IN THRILLER AND HORROR

Light and darkness have always been connoted as primary metaphors in film and television as the aesthetic equivalent of the opposition between 'good' and 'evil'. While light is associated with hope, happiness and community, darkness tends to mean insecurity, fear and loneliness. Uncanny things rarely happen in broad daylight; not for nothing does the absence of light generate greater potential for fear. It is therefore not surprising that the terrors from thriller and horror narratives preferably take place in the dark, regularly in the deepest night, because the greatest horror is still caused by danger that cannot be seen and instead can only be guessed at.

Light and darkness signal 'good' and 'evil' in film and television

It is not without reason that the blackout is a recurring standard motif in film and television entertainment when evil and terrifying things are going on. Monstrous figures and bloodthirsty criminals choose the cover of darkness to do their dirty work, or they simply create the blackout themselves to make their job easier. In any case, darkness always brings a shocking surprise effect – for the characters as well as for the audience in the cinema seats and on the sofa: the lurking 'bad' can exploit the guilelessness of its victims sitting in the dark to attack them and either kill them, eat them up or otherwise harass them. In cinematic art forms, a black-

The 'evil' has an easy game in the darkness of the blackout, because victims are largely defenseless

out is thus the ideal opportunity for all kinds of mischief and mischievousness, which the largely defenseless victims have to endure. Only the end of the blackout, the return of light and the protection of normality, as narratives of horror and thrillers tell it, can put an end to the terror.

The forms of horror that await in the blackout are as diverse as the films of the thriller and horror genres themselves: brutal murderers and bloodthirsty psychopaths, plagues of biblical proportions and diabolical figures straight from hell, soulless undead and homicidal mutants – they all unfold their greatest horror when the light switches don't work, no help can be phoned in and there is no place to take refuge. Often, it is quite 'worldly' dangers that descend upon their victims under the cover of the blackout. In the Danish-Swedish-German co-production *Broen* or *Bron* (*The Bridge*, 2011–2018), something strange happens in the pilot episode. On the Øresund Bridge, which connects Copenhagen in Denmark with Malmö in Sweden, the power goes out at midnight for exactly 48 seconds – triggered by remote access from a computer. Shortly thereafter, a woman's body is found lying exactly on the Danish-Swedish border – and here it starts to get complicated, because the homicide departments of both countries feel responsible. The case becomes even more difficult when they try to remove the body, because it turns out that there are actually two dead bodies, at least two 'half' corpses: the upper body belongs to a Swedish local politician, the lower body to a prostitute who has been missing in

> Blackout attracts 'worldly' horrors: murderers and psychopaths

Denmark for a long time. Exactly where the two halves of the body meet, the Danish-Swedish border runs, marked with a yellow line. In the course of the first season, the impression arises that the murderer wants to draw attention to various social grievances with his deeds, but in reality he is driven primarily by feelings of revenge. In any case, it is astonishing that the killer managed to stage the horrible 'still life' on the bridge in less than a minute – he certainly wouldn't have succeeded so well without the power outage.

The events on the Øresund Bridge are unpleasant, but curious murder cases are not uncommon in detective stories and thrillers, even at family entertainment prime time on Sunday evenings. Considerably more depressing, on the other hand, is the situation that power outages create in horror films, such as *The Purge* (USA 2013). The idea of the (commercially unexpectedly successful) film, which established an entire *Purge* franchise with several sequels and a TV series, is as simple as it is ingenious: in the fictional year 2022, as imagined a decade ago, a fascistic party calling itself "The New Founding Fathers of America" rules the United States. In order to keep crime and unemployment down in the country, the annual "Purge" was launched: for one night, any violent crime is then allowed, including murder; police and emergency services are unavailable and do not resume their work until the next morning. With foresight, certain weapons are banned and government employees from "level 10" (probably comparable to the German salary grade B) are not

In the blackout also and especially the 'good bourgeois' show their 'true face': anarchy looms

allowed to be involved in order to ensure the functioning of the state. The absurd strategy is said to have been 'successful' here in fiction, at least it is said to have helped people 'let their hair down' once a year so they could stay more peaceful the rest of the time, and damage control and private security firms would have generated many new jobs. "Tonight allows people a release for all the hatred and violence and aggression that they keep up inside them... You don't remember how bad it was, Charlie. The poverty, all the crimes. This night saved our country," (M18) the young son is told by his father. Strictly speaking, the "Purge" is a calculated 'civilizational blackout', a suspension of modernity for one night.

But the blackout also exists here in its pure manifestation. The father sells particularly safe (and profitable) houses that are supposed to scare of or at least discourage the killers – which unfortunately only works in 99 percent of the cases. The family, which has visibly profited from the father's many contract deals, also barricades itself behind its steel doors and its surveillance monitors every year. When the son gives refuge to a persecuted man in the bunker house, his perverse tormentors (who see in their murder victim only "a grotesque menace to our just society" and insist on their purge rights as 'free American citizens', M35) gradually grow impatient and demand extradition. They turn off the family's electricity to press their demands. Only the surveillance cameras are still working because they are on emergency power, and the wild flashlight

Perpetrators of violence use blackout as a means of pressure – and for a frightening atmosphere creates a not particularly cozy atmosphere in the armored mansion, which now turns out to be a potential death trap. Above all, the glaring backlight from the truck of the wealthy Purge friends (cf. fig. 25) lends the blackout scene an ominous mood. Finally, the occupied family is able to defend itself against the law-abiding killers, but the danger ends only with sunrise.

Figure 25: During The Purge *(M61), the intellectual wealthy are among the most disgusting butchers in the annual 'Purge' night. They use the combination of night and blackout, which is well-tried in horror films, in order to have an easy time with their victims on the one hand, and on the other hand to provide an eerie atmosphere for the purpose of an impressive appearance on stage.*

Because the film (somewhat heavy-handed despite its remarkable socio-critical concern) failed to fully exploit the potential of the radical idea, an entire *Purge* film universe has grown up (*The Purge: Anarchy,* 2014; *The Purge: Election Year,* 2016; *The First Purge,* 2018; *The Purge Forever,* 2021), with one film being more disturbing than the previous one. Blackouts are not to be missed here, not even

Blackout never does any good in horror, even when it first appears to do so in the television series *The Purge* (USA 2018–2019). Here, a group of deviant board members has retreated to a castle to commit systematic rapes (enjoying impunity in this absurd world). When the lights go out, the boss of the perverted corporate party becomes uneasy, because the power outage also means defenselessness for the monsters. As feared, an armed man in mask enters the place of torture and shoots those who participated in the repulsions. He appears like an unexpected savior in need. But the supposed liberator has his very own Purge plans: in a dungeon he gathers everyone who is supposed to have wronged him in some way in the course of his life – from a bully from school days to a date who turned him down to a random stranger who didn't thank him for opening the door. Purge night gives him the right to exact revenge on them – but as soon as daylight returns, the law-abiding citizen lets go of his victims. The series proves that there is no exception to the rule: the darkness of the blackout never brings anything good, but always only ruin.

This also applies to the supernatural and fantastic horrors that power outages bring in horror films from time to time. In the genre classic *The Fog* (USA 1980) by master John Carpenter, a small Californian coastal town has to dress warmly. At a midnight campfire, an old sea dog tells a visibly gripped group of children a horror story: a hundred years ago, a ship was wrecked on the shore because in the thick fog they mistook a campfire on the coast for

'Evil' often announces itself even before the actual danger by blackouts – forewarning allows preparation

the saving lighthouse. On this night, exactly a century after the seafaring disaster, the small town suddenly goes crazy: telephones ring and spew coins, supermarket shelves shake, gas pumps are leaking, cars honk, TVs and radios turn on. The chaos heralds greater doom, as shortly thereafter a mysterious glowing fog bank settles over the water, carrying with it the undead souls of sailors who once perished. A small boat crew is the first to fall victim to the astonishingly malignant fog and its inhabitants when it penetrates the generator and renders the boat unable to maneuver. Angry sailors descend on the boat from a large sailing vessel to lynch the three drunken fishermen. Just in time for the end of the 'witching hour', the fog (together with the ominous company) disappears again. There at Spivey Point, where the fateful bonfire once burned, now actually stands a lighthouse, from which a charming radio woman has a view of the town and presents her nightly show in a well-informed manner. She had still warned the boat crew about the fog that suddenly drifted away against the wind. The whole fog thing doesn't seem kosher to her when she learns of the disappearance of the three men the next day. It turns out that once upon a time, one hundred years ago, the sailors had fallen for a deadly conspiracy: the oh-so-honorable founding fathers of the village had deliberately let the leprous people on the ship steer against the rocks and seize their gold. Now the deceived have risen from the dead and want revenge

– which is easier without electricity. Again the un-
natural fog appears at night, this time heading for
the city.

When the radio host observes the strange spectacle on the water and hears the weatherman being
killed on the phone, she switches gears in a flash:
she has to warn the population! She first contacts
the sheriff via radio announcement, but then the
power goes out in the whole town: the fog has
shock-frozen the local power supply, paralyzing
communications throughout the town. Without
mass media, the town is initially defenseless against
the fog of horror. Now the small generator that the
radio woman keeps in the tower pays off. In her
concern for the well-being of the town and especially for her son, she could drive into the town to
save her child, but she is very aware of the special
function of a radio in such an emergency situation:
first fearfully, then composedly and pointedly, she
continuously relays the current position of the fog
that is gradually encircling the town (cf. fig. 26). She
warns: "Get inside and lock your doors! Close the
windows! There's something is in the fog!" (M73)
Following the instructions and directions of the radio host, people flee from the bloodthirsty sailors
through the darkness of the last unfogged streets
and save themselves in the local church, which is
here converted into a kind of disaster control center
as an emergency shelter. Eventually, the small radio
station is also enveloped by the murderous mist and
the generator fails, but until the host has to save herself on the roof of her lighthouse to fight one of the

Blackout interrupts
communication –
but radio continues
operations and
warns of danger in
real time

angry castaways, she is on air. With the conclusion of the revenge campaign, the haunting is over. After the battle, the dedicated radio voice returns to the microphone and, in tears, addresses the public once again in her capacity as makeshift 'disaster manager': "To the ships at sea who can hear my voice: Look across the water into the darkness! Look for the fog!" (M86) While the city is still in shock, the radio remains the only truly functioning social institution in the midst of the deadly blackout.

Figure 26: During the revenge attack by sailors returned from the grave in The Fog *(M67), the small local station KAB Radio 1340 in the lighthouse remains capable of broadcasting and can transmit potentially life-saving information to the population of Antonio Bay. In the blackout, the radio woman does not wait for further instructions from the authorities, but reacts with lightning speed and presence of mind to avert greater damage.*

The fog as a mixture of stylistic device, prop and backdrop was a genius idea by John Carpenter that still enjoys cult status today: the semi-transparent veils play with the visibility and invisibility of

Fog as a recurring cinematic device to stage darkness even in daylight the impending danger, and thus with the experience of safety and uncertainty. It is therefore to be expected that fog is frequently used in the genre to add another dimension of terror to the darkness typical of horror. In Steven King's novel *The Mist,* published like *The Fog* in 1980, things are also nebulous, although this time the beasts do not descend from the afterlife, but from another dimension as a result of military experiments. The setting is made for a television series that was produced in the U.S. in 2017, but canceled after one (somewhat bland) season. Because the creators of the series had probably expected a sequel, everything remains rather mysterious after the end of *The Mist's* first season. What seems indisputable is that the fog does not bring anything good here either. The inhabitants of the small town of Bridgeville in the northern coastal state of Maine carry their big and small problems around with them, as it should be in such a small town. While the people go about their daily lives quite grimly, an unusually thick fog rolls in. Through the windows of the local shopping center, nothing can be seen except the shallow white wall. It's daytime and bright in itself, but the fog has plunged the mall into nighttime darkness.

Of course, the power goes out and the great uncertainty begins. This is only intensified when those who leave the mall despite being warned are disfigured and killed by the fog. Since the police can no longer be reached by phone, they decide to barricade themselves in the mall. Unfortunately, the emergency communication set provided by the U.S.

Crisis communication only helpful if equipment is widely available and handling is practiced

Federal Emergency Management Agency (FEMA), including a CB radio and a satellite telephone terminal, is located in the foggiest section of the mall, where the first dead are already lying. The chosen ones make it to the equipment box and also the batteries are indeed charged, but unfortunately nobody answers 'on the other side'. The social tensions among the people trapped in the mall continue to increase, because there is no more water coming out of the tap and the console games, on which the young people gamble as if nothing had happened, are no fun in the long run without electricity.

The second half of the season is tiring: again and again the poor characters must flee from the fog in the darkness, because otherwise biblical plagues and an agonizing death threaten. All modern backdrops are enveloped is the cold weak light of flashlights and emergency lamps, which makes all faces look pale and bleak. Of course, the core of this story is less about hazy monsters than about their symbolic power as an anarchic, uncontrollable countervailing force to modernization and the carelessness of accustomed consumer affluence. It is not the mist that is producing the horrors in this world, but ultimately the people themselves make their situation worse through their own unreasonable actions, does not bode well for the case when modernity is under attack and each individual tries to save himself from the violence of the horror blackout – in case of doubt with monstrous social behavior.

Monstrous dangers as incarnation of anti-modernity – but humans only make it worse

Things get even darker in *Cloverfield* (USA 2008), when Manhattan is haunted by a Godzilla-like creature. The exact background remains unclear in the film, but the very successful promotional campaign suggests that Clover (also lovingly called "Clovie") had probably come to light during drilling on a Japanese oil platform and then, without a mother, landed in Manhattan – disoriented, lonely and frightened. While the New Yorkers are enjoying themselves at parties and unsuspectingly discussing more or less essential life issues (for example, an upcoming move to Japan, Clovie's home), the infantile monster makes its arrival unmistakably noticeable: through a small earthquake and finally through a city-wide power outage. The power supply is temporarily restored, but in the city, there is sheer horror. Again and again, all you can see of the primeval beast is an oversized tail (as big as the skyscrapers and bridges it knocks over, probably by accident) or a back that can withstand any bombardment by the Army and Air Force. Even if the emergency lighting in the eerily empty stores, subway stations and hallways provides some orientation, the panic-stricken fear of the helpless victims is transferred to the viewers. The emergency lighting, however, is a double-edged sword: on the one hand, it is helpful in preventing one from accidentally falling into a hole in the panic; on the other hand, it unmistakably signals an underlying apocalyptic mood. Especially in the scene of the makeshift hospital, which the Army has set up in the middle of a mall between glaring generator-driven spotlights, the emergency lighting

Aesthetic effects of the blackout transfer the characters' feelings of fear to the audience.

does not give a feeling of safety, but of calamity. The effect is reinforced by the pseudo-documentary style of the film, which narrates the events only through the tape footage from a protagonist's video camera. Because the tape must be repeatedly fast-forwarded and rewound to inspect Clovie and extract information about his behavior, shots of carefree times, such as a fun trip to Coney Island in Brooklyn, are repeatedly interspersed between images of the monster's attacks. As they sit on the Ferris Wheel – unaware of what's to come – the amateur cameraman's girlfriend sums up at the end of the tape: "I had a good day." (M74) The contrast with the last amateur shot, when the monster is taken out by bombardment in Central Park, could not be more intense.

Days without electricity are usually highly unpleasant for characters in film and television, especially in the horror genre. Cities, homes and businesses become death traps from which there is no escape. A popular plot location for blackout-driven cinematic horror narratives is, of course, the elevator: if the power fails, the passengers are not only imprisoned, but also have to endure with each other in a very confined space – not just for a minute, as planned, but potentially for hours: no one can avoid the other anymore – and not even themselves, their own thoughts and fears, which always travel along in the elevator. It goes without saying that friction can arise in this intensified social situation. In the appropriately titled film *Blackout* (USA 2008), for example, three people thrown together at random

Stuck elevator as a recurring plot point: forced break with strangers means danger

get stuck in an elevator when the power goes out in their apartment building. As flashbacks reveal, all three are in a terrible hurry: Claudia wants to fulfill a dying grandmother's last wish; Tommy wants to emigrate to Paris with his girlfriend, who was abused by her father, and she is probably already waiting impatiently for him; Karl is a doctor and, in his spare time, a psychopathic serial killer who commits sadistic murders of women and wants to quickly remove the traces of the previous evening before his daughter comes to visit him. The latter initially makes the calmest impression of all: as a doctor, he is used to stressful situations, jokes around as if he were on rounds, and seems surprisingly relaxed. However, the longer the elevator is stuck and the greater the risk of his exposure as a murderer, the more he shows his insane side, threatening the other two fellow sufferers and ultimately trying to kill them. In the end, only Claudia survives the terrifying ride in the elevator. Without the blackout, all three characters would have gone their separate ways again after a brief moment of chance encounter, but the blackout forces an interruption of the short-term life plans of all three fellow travelers: they have to pay for the unexpected forced break from the accelerated modern everyday life with a confrontation with the repressed truth of their habits and way of living. This is also the fate of the five unfortunates who have to face the incarnation of the *Devil* (USA 2010) in the form of a previously warm-hearted elderly lady when they are in an elevator: they are all eliminated one after the other until only one last passenger, burdened with heavy feelings of guilt, is left. Without the blackout, he would probably never have met the policeman whose family he had negligently killed in a hit-and-run accident, but now he gets the opportunity to do so during the blackout.

Supernatural creatures and malicious alien beings make the majority of blackout-causing phenomena in the horror genre: zombies, mutants and aliens form a successful trio, whose activity always reliably leads to a blackout. When modern society is overrun by the undead with an appetite for brains, previously peaceful citizens who have mutated into monsters, or aliens with dubious motives, the collapse of modern institutions is usually recognizable by a widespread power outage: zombies and mutants are just not known to reliably control power plants, maintain transformer stations, or bring in fuel; aliens, on the other hand, often come with technology far superior to human development, capable of knocking out all the electrical wonders of the world with a snap of their fingers (if the creatures have fingers at all). It is from their destructive power, directed against modernization, that the probable terror of these creatures emanates; as incarnations of anti-modernity, they embody (despite their fantastic appearance) quite 'secular' problems: the fear that electrified modernity might turn against itself.

Zombies, mutants, aliens as the main cause of horror blackouts: modernity has no chance against them

At the beginning of *Dawn of the Dead* (USA 2004), nurse Ann has just returned from a strenuous shift at the clinic, but there is still enough motivation for a passionate shower with her husband, while the TV is on in the background: the current program is interrupted by a special broadcast – which the two have fatally missed. The next morning, the neighbor's daughter is in the bedroom, biting the husband, turning him into a zombie, who in turn unexpectedly viciously attacks the wife. The phone does not work, she is on her own. At the last second, she manages to escape through the bathroom window into the car, and the radio is already broadcasting the official information about where the nearest evacuation centers are located. The couple can't be blamed for turning their backs on the TV after their exhausting day. The director's cut, however, sets the action a bit earlier and shows Ann at the end of her shift, which only exacerbates the unfortunate initial situation. In the hospital, a patient with a bite wound is already lying in the intensive care unit, strangely dangerous-feeling announcements are coming over the radio, and the young woman prefers to turn off the radio station with the news, which is just reporting on increasing mysterious violent excesses, in favor of the song *Have a Nice Day*, which is less stressful. The audience – knowing, thanks to the film's title, that the tranquility of the peaceful suburb isn't likely to last much longer – is entitled to feel justifiably superior: the main character could have known better; after all, the warning signs were everywhere. The fact

Characters in horror do not take indications of impending horror seriously enough

that she then wakes up the next morning completely clueless will be her and her husband's undoing.

The characters who run into the open knife in *Fear the Walking Dead* fare similarly: Nick, a drug addict with a penchant for hallucinations, can't trust his own memories after having to flee from a cannibalistic junkie; the school bus is only a third full because some 'flu' is going around; videos show dead accident victims bitingly attacking their paramedics; civil war-like conditions prevail downtown. Things escalate quickly, but not abruptly. However, because no one thinks it possible that in just a few hours the electricity will be gone and modernity will be in danger, life with all its banal problems continues as if nothing had happened.

Blackout never comes out of nowhere – but lack of awareness of possibility of anti-modernity creates overstress

But sometimes in the horror genre, things move faster than you can shift gears. In *#Alive* (*#Saraitda*, KR 2020), the impending zombie apocalypse sets a respectable pace: Junu has just been role-playing on the computer when his comrades-in-arms urge him to turn on the TV: "Is that for real? That's CGI." (M03) The news reports of a rapidly spreading virus that is making people pretty aggressive. At the same moment, a disaster warning appears on the smartphone via cell broadcast; outside, all hell is breaking loose over the city. The telephone network is overloaded, the TV program keeps dropping out. After an infected neighbor enters his apartment, directly turning into a zombie. Junu decides to *survive*: he follows the official instructions from the

Tips from trusted acquaintances, television news and cell broadcast are in combination clear warning

television, as his mum told him to, explores the situation with the help of a drone and barricades himself behind taped window panes at home.

But his supplies quickly run out (cf. fig. 27), no more drops of water come out of the taps and because he has no wired headphone, he can't listen to the radio with his smartphone – and thus he cannot receive official disaster reports ("Damn it. Why are they all wireless [these days]?" M29). When he learns that his family has probably been carried off by the undead, he loses all hope – but he only makes his decision to commit suicide after the inevitable blackout, which here doesn't set in until 38 minutes into the film. He is lucky that a neighbor in the house opposite observes the events and points out his 'idiotic' behavior. Because they sent out their location on social media right at the beginning of the disaster with the hashtag *#I_must_survive*, the disaster management agency manages to rescue the few survivors from their homes at the end. The high school students from the teen zombie series *All of Us Are Dead* (KR 2022) will not have this luck: they may remember that in disaster movies, the military would always come and save everyone: "At least there are cops and soldiers out there, right?" – "But if you watch the movies, they can't do anything, either, right?" – "Yeah, but they always save everyone in the end." (S01E04M17) However, the government in this fictional grotesque decides to sacrifice the capital to save the rest of the country. Finally, the zombie blackouts lead directly into a post-electrical age in which humans must not only defend

Power supply failure leads characters to brink of despair as belief in rescue fades

themselves against the biting undead, but also completely reorganize their lives without electricity.

Figure 27: Supplies for the fight against the zombie apocalypse are gradually running low in #Alive (M53). At least it gives the lonely gamer strength that he doesn't have to eat his last noodle soup all alone, because via walkie talkie the lost main character finds unexpected contact with a survivor on the other side of the street.

If anyone can match the destructive energy of movie and TV zombies, it's mutants, whose monstrous power brings society to a standstill so quickly that modernity, and with it electrification, collapses like a house of cards. In the (not coincidentally also Korean) series *Sweet Home* (2020), the residents of an apartment building are trapped when more and more brutal monsters appear outside – one uglier than the other. At first the phones don't work anymore, the emergency call is overloaded, only the disaster warning of the authorities comes through the line: in case of mutation into a giant monster you should stay at home and isolate yourself. The

Modernity is completely defenseless against the horror mutants

brutal manager of the supermarket, on the other hand, is more concerned about the melting frozen goods, but he doesn't want to give them away for free, despite the apocalyptic conditions in the apartment building – he'd rather throw them away. The characters initially hope that the problem will be reduced to their apartment building. However, during a television broadcast of the president, which is supposed to serve the purpose of reassurance ("The government is working hard to keep us safe", S01E03M14), he too turns into one of the monsters ("Everyone is going to die!", S01E03M15) and is shot on camera, then there is only a test image. The next day, the interim government declares a state of emergency, but is also unsuccessful in its efforts to soothe them: "Survive out there. And good luck to us all." (S01E04M15) Mutants tear the modern age to pieces.

In *Wayward Pines* (USA 2015–2016), which at first glance seems idyllic, but in reality is highly mysterious, the world seems to have stood still at some point in America's Golden Age. In fact, however, it is not an inconspicuous small town in the middle of nowhere, but a kind of 'Noah's Ark' in the year 4028: at the beginning of the 21st century, a scientist somewhere between genius and madness had realized that sooner or later (as a result of climate change, pollutants and other present-day catastrophes) humanity would mutate into beasts and Homo Sapiens would become extinct in its modern form. Hundreds of mostly unsuspecting fellow human beings were frozen, only to be thawed out two

> Modernity protects against dangers through electricity – blackout makes life too easy for the anti-modern forces

thousand years later. They now populate the small town of *Wayward Pines*, protected by an electric fence from what Prophet Pilcher had foreseen: the 'Abbies', whose genetic mutations make the surrounding area unsafe with an insatiable appetite and remarkable bite. If the first generation of the reawakened was still freaked out in the face of the truth, Pilcher decided in the second attempt to leave the population better uninformed and for the sake of simplicity to deter people with death penalties in case of *wayward*ness. Much civilization is not left here. When the citizens become rebellious at the finale of the first season (S01E10) and the secret slips away from him, Pilcher – knowing full well that he still has a few shock-frosted ones in reserve – tries to help the downfall of the city a bit and deactivates the electric fence. As expected, the 'Abbies' attack the little town, which can only save itself with its last ounce of strength (cf. fig. 28).

This leads to two important cues. First, in the event of a confrontation with rabid mutants, an electrical safety fence should be adequately secured against accidental and intentional shutdown. Second, since cryopreservation procedures may become even more popular in the coming decades and premature defrosting of the frozen would jeopardize their later resuscitation and thus their social reintegration, providers of such services would be well advised to install a doomsday resilient power supply that continues to run even after the power plant employees have already been eaten by the expected mutants or other anti-modern aggressors.

Future technologies and protective devices particularly dependent on electricity – precautions necessary

Figure 28: Without the protective electric fence, the inhabitants of Wayward Pines *(S01E10M11) are at the mercy of the aggressive mutants. They take advantage of the darkness to jump at the victims from every obscured corner.*

Finally, the aliens remain as sources for the blackout. When they are visiting the humans, this usually has two backgrounds. During the classic *Close Encounters of the Third Kind* (USA 1977) all devices go crazy at the first arrival of the aliens, they switch *on,* before it comes to the big blackout. The aliens are all in all well-disposed towards the humans and in the end even take some specimens of our kind with them on a journey to their distant home in a spaceship. Obviously, the blackout serves no hostile purpose here, but is meant to attract attention: it signals to humans that strange things are about to happen. Often the beings from alien worlds visit the Earth and its inhabitants not for reasons of friendship between peoples, but want to subjugate

Aliens eliminate power supply accidentally or intentionally – works efficiently as modernization destruction and attentional control mechanism

mankind and take the fruitful planet for themselves. Here, too, a blackout lends itself to organizing the elimination of humanity more efficiently. In the Moscow of *The Darkest Hour* (USA 2011), the doom begins with the arrived aliens being able to produce local and area-wide blackouts at will. Similarly, in a reinterpretation for television of H. G. Wells' classic *War of the* Worlds (USA/FR 2019), the colonialist aliens deploy powerful electromagnetic radiation that kills two birds with one stone: all humans who are not in a heavily armored shelter at the time die instantly, and those who are holed up somewhere would probably perish eventually because the global EMP turned off all electrical devices. The 'rest' are taken care of by the four-legged semi-automatic dog-like killing machines. Under these conditions the people have hardly a chance: without electricity the world is easier to subjugate. Moreover, the world is hit completely unprepared, so there is no possibility to get ready for the invasion in any form.

The inhabitants of the small town of Chester's Mill, which disappears under a mysterious invisible dome and is cut off from the outside world from one moment to the next, seem to be in a comparatively good position *Under The Dome (*USA 2013–2015). Apart from its own small local radio station, there is no longer any broadcasting. Smartphones don't work either because the dome shields all signals. The tech-savvy master's student in electrical engineering who works at the local station manages to pick up fragments of information from the world

Self-sufficient municipal power supply arms against possible bottlenecks and global crisis

beyond the dome through some trickery, but the town is on its own. Fortunately, the small city has the local radio station, from where important emergency announcements are made by the dodgy and self-important (but at least initially quite dutiful) town councilman James "Big Jim" Rennie – for example, that all vehicles should stop immediately to avoid smashing into the invisible outer wall of the dome. However, as the city council with its dark secrets resorts to ever more blatant means of maintaining power in the course of the first season and also abuses the radio for its propaganda purposes, the tremendous importance of a free press becomes apparent. Official emergency announcements should obviously be limited, in accordance with legal norms, to absolute emergencies in which there is imminent danger – official or state control of broadcasting, however, would be a serious interference in the free opinion-forming process. Among the village's well-kept secrets are its considerable supplies of propane gas, which actually serve the local drug industry but now provide a measure of security during foreclosure and the compulsion to be self-sufficient. Intelligent Joe is also lucky enough to have a generator at his parents' house. When word gets out that he can charge your smartphone so you can finally at least listen to some music again, this attracts the entire village youth, including some charming girls. At the same time, however, distribution battles begin when the king of the schoolyard occupies the power strip and demands money for every charge.

Only an overload of the generator puts an end to the occupation monopoly (cf. fig. 29).

Figure 29: In times of blackout, the generator becomes a status monopoly, at least as long as you have fuel and it doesn't run down, as here in Under The Dome *(S01E03M38). It can be used to recharge the mementos of bygone modern times, smartphones for example, which have long since ceased to be useful for making phone calls, but are nowadays the only photo album that many still own.*

The initial situation in the teen drama *The Society* (USA 2019) is quite similar, even if the aliens can't be blamed here. The actual cause for the predicament, which also ultimately leads to a blackout here, is not explained in the first season, but the situation of the characters is unfortunate in any case: when the youth of a small Connecticut town return early from a school trip due to impassable roads, all the adults at home have disappeared. The young

Blackout gradually dissolves minimal social consensus and threatens sense-making

people gradually understand that they can neither leave the town nor communicate with the outside world. For some surprising reason, however, they can still be in contact with each other within the town by smartphone, and although there is no one to produce it, electricity continues to come out of the socket. However, concern grows that this might not last forever when, during a boisterous house party, the lights suddenly begin to flicker and the awareness sets in that an iPhone's battery, and thus the lamp in the cell phone, won't last forever. From here on, social decay sets in and progresses swiftly and dramatically: a dictatorial form of rule emerges in the powerless town as the high school jocks, who previously served as a makeshift police force, now stage a coup against the democratic emergency order. In this world, the terror emanating from the blackout is more subtle than elsewhere in the genre: hardly anyone feels bound by a social contract in this world left to its own devices. Everything becomes arbitrary, truth is interchangeable. In a remarkable philosophical excursion in the conversation between democratic and terrorist athletes, basic constructivist ideas can be found, for when everything becomes indifferent, when there is no longer a minimum social consensus, such as a transparent distribution of roles, an anarchy of meaning threatens: "Because from now on, we decide what everything means." (S01E10M23)

This loss of meaning and thus of the delicate fabric of social trust is probably the greatest source of the horror that threatens in the blackout films

Horror of the loss of modernity leads to bondless postmodernity and series: with the blackout, the bond to modernity and its laws, and thus the perceived obligation to act in an appropriate modern way, threatens to be lost. Horror arises when modernity threatens to disappear, and with it: the modern social contract. Blackout as an anti-modern force provides the ideal conditions for this. If the decay cannot be stopped in time, the figures of these scenarios end up in a switched-off post-modernity that functions according to completely different rules.

8. BLACKOUT AS APOCALYPSE: LIFE IN THE DE-ELECTRIFIED WORLD

An ordinary power outage temporarily upsets the familiar modern routines of life when coffee machines no longer work, the elevator stops running and the toilet no longer flushes. But the inconvenience will come to an end as soon as the power sockets spit out the lifeblood of modern society again – normality returns. In the event of a widespread and prolonged power outage, a blackout, on the other hand, it is uncertain whether a quick return to the accustomed modern living conditions will be possible – or whether the absence of electricity might even become the new normality. In most films and TV series that deal with blackouts, the fictional narrative world succeeds in eliminating the causes of the disruption and restoring the original state as far as possible. With the onset of the blackout, a race against time begins, as the damage increases more and more as the catastrophe progresses, until a return to modernity gradually becomes less and less likely.

Blackout damage increases exponentially over time – and quickly becomes unrecoverable

If one believes the scenarios of film and television, it takes only a few weeks, sometimes just a few days, to exorcise modernity from the world through a blackout: because at a certain point – similar to the 'tipping points' feared in the wake of climate change – certain spirals of escalation can no longer be reversed and the consequential damage exceeds society's ability to eliminate it, a blackout

Blackout can set in motion escalating spirals of irreversible demodernization

can push modernity to its limits. If, for example, the consequences to be dealt with by a nationwide power blackout exceed a certain level of reasonableness for the individual, and self-protection takes effect that prevents employees (such as public servants, police and firefighters, or power plant and power grid workers) from still showing up for work, and modern services are thus no longer available, cascading effects arise: the causes responsible for their onset in the first place intensify ever more rapidly. The tight network of social dependency becomes porous and gradually dissolves – and with it, modernity with its high degree of division of labor gets destabilized. Only if it is possible to intervene in time in the early phase of the blackout and stop the self-reinforcing decay, a transition to post-modernity can be prevented. Otherwise, the blackout-ridden world will dissolve and will be released in a post-electrified post-modernity.

The Netflix film *Awake* (USA 2021) shows an interesting idea to illustrate this connection. Here, unusually strong solar flares lead to a problematic double effect. On the one hand, all electronic devices and the power supply fail: nothing that has a chip or depends on electricity still works, even satellites and airplanes fall from the sky. On the other hand – and this is arguably even more serious – no one can fall asleep once the blackout begins: the solar storm has affected human "electromagnetic wiring, it affected our glymphatic system" (M73) and thus human biorhythms. While the whole of man-

Modern society can last about as long without electricity as a person can without sleep

kind is struggling with chronic overtiredness, increasingly suffering from exhaustion syndromes and gradually being plagued by delusions and aggressiveness, only a few people in the world can still find nightly rest, namely those who have survived a clinical death, probably because this resets their 'internal clock'. Thus the time of mankind is running out: only if a cure can be found in time – as long as the stimulant cocktails delay the inevitable and enough researchers, military personnel and government people are still able to work at all – the downfall of human civilization can still be stopped. The constellation is remarkable because the two problems – the technology blackout and the insomnia – produce similar difficulties: just as during a blackout all refrigerators, hospitals and communication networks can only be kept alive temporarily with generators and batteries, the insomniacs face a similar inevitable fate when the last energy reserves are exhausted. Surprisingly, the time that looms after the onset of a blackout until societal 'brain death' is comparable to that left to involuntarily awake humanity: "After 48 hours of no sleep, there's a loss of critical thinking. 96 hours: hallucinations, motor failure. But what about after that? Organs will fail, but then what? Days of lying in paralysis until the heart shuts off?" (M18) This description applies in a frightening way just as well to a modern society on the way of its de-electrization: one could also replace the word "sleep" with "electricity" in the researcher's description and the statement would be just as true. Just like a life without sleep, a modern society without electricity becomes more fragile with every hour, and finally proves to be deadly – for the individual as well as for modernity in general.

Figure 30: In Awake *(M44), there are no working computers since the blackout. The doomed mother prepares her daughter for life in a de-electrified age: "This is gonna be your new school. So, when mommy's gone, you'll need to find a library. ... And read, don't stop reading."*

If the problem cannot be dealt with in time, modernity will be threatened with death by exhaustion, because without electricity it will quickly reach the limits of its endurance, just like a person without sleep. *Awake* finds a strong allegory for this: once a certain 'point of no return' has been passed, the threat of relapse into a de-electrified post-modernity looms. The main heroine, a former military officer with drug problems, sets herself up for the decline of civilization – because her ten-year-old daughter is one of the few people who can still

In the post-modern era, it pays to have analog alternatives for important services sleep. After the end of the modern world, who will raise her, take care of her? Suddenly, everything that works without electricity becomes important here: the analog card catalog in the library, a printed street map for navigating, a vintage car without circuits that could burn out (cf. fig. 30). The worried mother insists that the daughter learns to acquire knowledge without a computer, to research in books how to shoot animals herself, and to learn how to handle a gun – even if a weapon has no place in the hands of a child. Anything without electronics is of particular use in the upcoming post-modern era: valuables that can be traded even when credit card terminals no longer work and cash is meaningless, mechanical locks that remain closed even when central bolting mechanisms in prisons go belly up, printed research papers that in modern times existed as as immaterial data traces on now 'fried' servers. By sheer coincidence, they manage to find the solution to the problem just before their time runs out – cynically, it takes the power of defibrillators to do so. What luck that the resuscitators have a strong battery.

At the end of *Awake,* it remains unclear whether there is enough modernity left to leave the path to post-modernity at the last second. Even in *World War Z*, where in the midst of the zombie apocalypse telephone calls can only be made via satellite connection (cf. fig. 31), or in the world of *How It Ends,* which is shrouded in ashes, it is impossible to say whether the life expectancy of modernity has already passed or whether it will be

Characters from blackout fictions tormented by uncertainty whether modernity can be saved at all in the end given a reprieve. In *Transcendence* (USA 2014), on the other hand, the electrified world is deliberately sacrificed to stop the preparation of a (sinister but actually very useful) nanorobot technology: the virus-initiated blackout leads directly to a dark age in which laptops are used only as doorstops – but there remains a spark of hope that the few surviving nanobots might once pave the way for a return to an electrified age.

Figure 31: For the wife of the heroic zombie liquidator (Brad Pitt) left behind on the aircraft carrier, the satellite phone is the last connection to her beloved, because during World War Z *(M78) nothing else works anymore, smartphones are just expensive Gameboys. The satellite phone becomes the last functioning medium of the modern world (which of course only works in the open air).*

But sometimes in film and television, modernity cannot be saved. The passengers of the endless flight *Into the Night* (BE 2020–) know that only a few people worldwide are likely to have survived the murderous solar storm and that there will be no return to normality: even looting the international seed bank that actually exists on Spitsbergen is of no

Solar storms, war, pandemics: Global catastrophes trigger unwinding of modernity

use if there's no one left to sow anything. *Dawn of the Planet of the Apes* (USA 2014) picks up at the end of the first part of the Apes trilogy, after a pharmaceutical experiment wipes out the humans, while the Alzheimer's drug helps the hairy relatives gain unexpected intelligence. As governments around the world collapse, reactors melt down and the world's last lights go out, a thoughtful reporter comments: "So, maybe this is it. This is how it ends. Pretty soon there won't be anyone left." (M03) There is no going back to modernity. It is the dawn of post-modernity.

Feature films and television series that start from the end-time premise of complete demodernization and thus also complete de-electrification have been heaping up for some time. Again and again, the few remaining survivors have to settle down in this uninhabitable post-apocalyptic world, which is especially unpleasant if you are old enough to still remember well the advantages of modern life. Three decades after a devastating third world war, the planet in *The Book of Eli* (USA 2010) is completely devastated and burned. In search of the last drops of drinking water, the last humans crawling across a desolate desert world full of gangs, speculators and would-be dictators. The only things of value here are those necessary for survival and left over from modern times, such as the last little bottle of shampoo with which the aspiring despot might wash his wife's hair one last time (cf. fig. 32). Living in this world is hard work every second – but life still goes on somehow even with the end of the

Characters in post-electric age live off remnants of modernity, post-modern way of life as a constant burden

electrified age. The few people who still exist in this world (with low pre-modern life expectancy) have to come to terms with their new uncomfortable post-modern home – they only have this one world after all.

Figure 32: To charge an old battery that can power an iPod and listen to How Can You Mend A Broken Heart *from modern times, the prophet of* The Book of Eli *(M23) has to dig deep into his pockets. The merchant is not impressed with the lighter, he wants grease pencils for lips, and toys. For three old KFC refreshment tissues, however, he lets himself be persuaded.*

The hit series *The Walking Dead* (USA 2010–2021) and *Fear the Walking Dead* (USA 2015–), for example, tell of a gradual deterioration of modern society due to an uncontrollable disease that turns people into biting zombies – even after their death: the wandering dead with no morals and a lust for killing become a permanent danger that makes the world almost uninhabitable. In the first seasons such narrative moments occur again and again, with which the demodernization irreversibly sets in. Even

Dissolution of the last modern institutions through streamlessness signals end of modernity as a whole when the "dead", as they are sometimes euphemistically called, are already running through the streets and anarchic conditions prevail, a hope remains palpable in the first episodes of *Fear the Walking Dead* that the problem could still be overcome with the help of modern institutions (military) and conflict resolution methods (domestic isolation in the suburb). With the blackout (S01E03, cf. chapter 5), however, this hope is practically exhausted. In *The Walking Dead*, on the other hand, the characters tie their belief in a future for the modern age to the CDC, the U.S. Centers for Disease Control, which should surely be best prepared for such a situation. Indeed, after fighting their way through more and more zombie mobs in a powerless world and making it all the way to Atlanta, the group finds a lone last researcher in the bunker-like sealed off research facility who is able to work on an antidote thanks to his own large emergency power supply. His motivation, however, is limited despite his willingness to sacrifice himself: for some time now, his colleagues in the foreign health authorities have stopped answering his calls (the French were the last survivors, but they "ran out of juice", S01E06M28), his most important samples have been destroyed by the fully automated laboratory as a precaution, and now the gas is gradually drying up in the hermetically sealed facility: "The world runs on fossil fuel. I mean, how stupid is that?" (S01E06M28) says the researcher to his exhausted guests, because when the generators have nothing left to burn, the facility goes into self-destruct mode. For foolproof illustration, an oversized clock shows a countdown. The last scientist waxes philosophical in the face of the impending blackout: "We always think there's gonna be more time. Then it runs out" (S01E06M27) – exactly when the lights and AC turn off.

The researcher now faces the impending death at 6,000 degrees almost with a sense of redemption: "No pain, an end to sorrow, grief, regret. Everything." (S01E06M31) This is probably to be taken literally, because with the devastating pandemic and the global total blackout caused by it, not only modernity ends here, but humanity as a whole, at least hardly anything of it remains except cold ruins, zombies and a handful of survivors. Although the trapped people manage to escape from the CDC in the self-destruction program, the hoped-for chance to fight their way through post-modernity will end in eleven exhausting seasons (exhausting for the characters as well as the audience), in which the joyful moments in the life of the characters can be counted on one hand. But because the collective need for an aesthetic confrontation with the anti-modern, which is embodied by the zombies and their violence, is still strong, one can already look forward (if one has enjoyed the escapism into the post-modern from the comfort of the modern sofa) to several spin-offs, such as the anthology series *Tales of the Walking Dead*. After all, it's hard to tell a story that hasn't yet begun: it's the history that follows after modern history ends.

> Narratives of the post-electric age enable 'safe' engagement with the threat of post-modernity

Television programs and streaming libraries are filled to the brim with these literal *post-modern* narratives that exude lasting fascination: having to settle into post-modernity because there is little left of our modern way of living, yet life must somehow be organized. This is the main concern of the many end-times narratives in film and television that tell of civilization's regression into a powerless age in the wake of a pandemic, technological collapse, or for mysterious reasons. It is no coincidence that such stories are often told through the perspective of young people: they have either already been born after the fall of modernity and know life from before only indirectly from reports of their elders, which become loaded into mythical narratives, or they have at most fragmentary memories of their own of life before the onset of post-modernity.

Young people in the powerless post-modern age gradually lose memory of modernity, which becomes a myth

Will modernity end in the foreseeable future? Will human civilization wither along with modernity? Or is life still possible in an electricity-free, post-modern, 'post-apocalyptic' world? These are precisely the questions that plague the young people of *The Walking Dead: World Beyond* (USA 2020–2021): they experienced the demise of the modern world only half-consciously as children and have since been raised well protected behind high walls in an self-sufficient commune. During these ten years on their island of bliss, they have had no contact with the 'dead' so far; instead, they go to a kind of high school, democratically elect their representatives and forge alliances with other "republics" (which, unfortunately, sometimes turn out to be

Sealed off pseudo-modern life amid de-electrified age suggests normalcy under post-apocalyptic circumstances

imperialistic). There's even some electricity in the modern-looking Campus Colony, though it's tedious to somehow keep a 10,000-person city running on decades-old solar technology. Since here, too, every dying person turns into a zombie, counter-modernization can't be locked away completely, but it can be kept under control, at least temporarily, with the help of bars on the doors of the elderly. With all this, the young people could build a kind of neo-modernity. But can such an trouble-free oasis, as already existed in the form of the prison turned commune in *The Walking Dead* or the Broke Jaw Ranch run by shady preppers in *Fear the Walking Dead,* really be maintained permanently against the general trend toward demodernization?

This serial world where a global blackout has devastated society suggests that the odds are low, and that it doesn't necessarily have to be a problem either. When someone in the titular *World Beyond* ('beyond' the borders of the Campus) needs help, a group of four teenagers embark on an uncertain journey, entering for the first time the no man's land populated and ruled by the soulless. As they make their way through the dead world full of wrecked cars, they first realize how time-consuming it is to disable the zombies, especially if you lack practice – yet they are curious, knowing that (unlike their Elysium) this is now their *true* world: a world of lifeless ruins. Where they once had piano lessons, a meter-deep hole juts into the street (cf. fig. 33), and bums no longer sit at the roadside, but the soulless, where bees have already nested. Looking at this world, one

Young people facing a post-modern life are increasingly coming to terms with their fate as the "last generation"

of the young people declares that humanity has perhaps 15 years left before extinction – and smiles serenely: "It's just how it is." (S01E02M12) Although they have their fenced-off neo-modern home, they seem resigned to the fact that they are among the "Endlings", the last generation of humans on earth: "That makes us special. I'm lucky to know that. To know that I need to make my life count." (S01E02M34)

Figure 33: All that's left of the music school is ruins. The young people of The Walking Dead: World Beyond *(S01E02M05) must make their peace with the end of modernity in order to live on in the new post-modern reality.*

Precisely because of this *memento mori,* they enjoy the last remnants of modern life: they may be the last people to get something out of it. When they spend the night in a tree house for better protection from the undead, for example, they make up for a

Makeshift modernity can only temporarily suspend forces of counter-modernity, but never entirely

bit of childhood that was robbed from them by the end of the world: they play with a bowling ball, a lighter, with a Monopoly game – and grab the utility property 'Electric Company' there as quickly as possible. But the gradually fading memories of the horror of doom, of the "Night the Sky Fell", cannot be entirely dispelled. Even if this 'last generation' in fiction manages to counter the de-electrified age with walkie talkies, solar cells and flashlights, these stopgap solutions cannot distract from the reality of the horror beyond the walls, such as the fact that a zombie here always comes around the corner just when the batteries have just run out (S01E03M11). It is just not possible to completely eliminate the soulless human shells, which are raging against everything orderly, rational – against modernity's rests. Even after ten years, the brain-dead biting bodies here still do not run out of energy to appear as an embodied metaphor of the modernization counterforces. Apparently, the counter-moderns continue to do their damage even when there is nothing left to fight against. This makes a return to modern conditions practically impossible.

In *The Walking Dead: World Beyond,* the young people at least have enough time to mentally adjust to the impending end and gradually wean themselves off modernity, even if the onset of civilizational decline came as a surprise. The young people in *Sløborn* (D 2020–), on the other hand, are still too mentally entrenched in modern life to be able to accept the new reality of life yet. The fictional North Frisian island becomes the focal point of the

Gradual withdrawal from modernity can help to cope better with new life situation, otherwise psychological overstretching

emerging pigeon flu, which increasingly develops into a devastating pandemic with high mortality during the first season. After the outbreak of the virus, the island is all but deserted, with only the few young people who managed to hide from evacuations to the mainland remaining. Four months after the emergency television broadcasts by the German Federal Office of Civil Protection and Disaster Assistance were cut short, the plot of Season 2 kicks in – with a blackout just in the first episode, inescapably titled "Alles anders" ("Everything has changed"). If the island still had electricity up to this point (the young *Sløborns* assume that the power plants on the mainland must run fully automatically), the last food in the refrigerators and freezers now threatens to spoil, the electronically locked doors no longer open (resulting in breakneck climbs) and the bestselling author has to type his first post-apocalyptic novel on a typewriter: "A sense of boundless emptiness. A completely new feeling: we don't know if we are alone. ... In my knowledge of the world, I resemble Stone Age man, who knew as much about the nature of the planet as he could see with his own eyes. And perhaps the new age has more in common with the Stone Age than we would like." (S02E01M42; own translation) Indeed, the powerless people on *Sløborn* are cut off from the outside world and any information about the state of the world: here, too, uncertainty about the whereabouts of the remaining nearly eight billion people becomes an existential burden.

When living through an apocalyptic phase, sitting on an island brings a certain security in the short term, but in the long term the seclusion leads to the problem that modernity, or at least a remnant of it, may still exist outside. This is also the source of the nightmares of the underage Evelin, who shortly before the outbreak of the pandemic has become pregnant. During the day she tries to acquire the necessary gynecological knowledge from library books, does her subsonic examinations herself and signs the pictures off the monitor by hand (she is out of printer paper). In her sleep she encounters the horror of having to give birth to her child without professional help, with only the novelist and a classmate providing support with panicked expressions on their faces; the child is deformed (S02E02M02). Fearing a miscarriage, a return to modernity is inevitable for the strong young woman: together with her brothers and the helpful writer, who takes the orphans into his care and equips their house with a large emergency generator and fuel (salvaged with a hand pump from the floor storage of a gas station), she contacts the hospital on the mainland via the harbor's emergency-powered radio system and plans an escape from the island.

Young people accustomed to modernity fear helplessness – escape back to civilization from last strength

For the majority of the other young people on *Sløborn*, who had come to the vacation paradise to escape a prison sentence for a resocialization project, the pandemic seems to have come at the right time: the lonely ones simply live in the day, enjoy the idyllic view on the beach and repeatedly run amok with fast cars, alcohol and drugs – often with

Embracing postmodernity or speculating on the return of modernity? Different attitudes lead to conflicts

devastating consequences. The main disagreement is whether this is really "the apocalypse" or merely a "respite, we needed it anyway" (S02E01M23; own translation); perhaps the pandemic is even an overdue 'reboot' for an overpopulated world with food problems and climate change caused by too much consumption (S02E03M34). Despite the hopeless situation, the leader of the reintegration project is meticulous about continuing to respect modern social rules: when the group stays in an abandoned hotel, takes groceries from a supermarket, or borrows a seemingly abandoned bicycle, the trainer leaves a list of the goods and services used along with her business card – as a billing address when checks are once again written. The anger that this psychological coping strategy, bordering on a loss of reality, triggers in the young people is understandable in a certain sense: "Stop pretending that this will all go away. As if it's just a little unforeseen incident and everything will go *back to normal* afterwards," one of the offenders, who is no longer willing to wait unfoundedly for modernity to return, gets angry – he wants and needs to accept the new reality in order to be able to go on living (S02E01M24; own translation). Others, on the contrary, cling convulsively to the past because the present is not an alternative worth living for them. Hermann, for example, repeatedly has a hallucination of his dead father, whom he once deliberately infected with the virus in order to free himself from his mistreatment. Now he suffers from strong feelings of guilt, which lead to a psychotic imagination that his father is still alive – while his decomposed corpse is lying at his home. He can only free himself from the paranoia that his father will continue to bully him when he reaches the mainland with the other young people and thus returns to the rest of modernity – then he no longer needs the ghost of the dead modernization rejecter.

The dandy writer, in turn, is well aware that there is probably no readership for his book anymore, but his existence has meaning only in a (at least imagined) modern context: "I write because I have to. You know, it stops time." (S02E02M17; own translation) In the meantime, Evelin lets the author teach her the most modern thing par excellence: driving a car. The blinker is also set, even and especially when no one sees it at all. The clever big sister also sees no reason to deprive her younger brothers of the hope of a return to normality and thus also of a reunion with their beloved parents; on the contrary: together with them, she writes letters to Mom and Dad. Even if they cannot send them, the mere formulation of the letters has an emotionally relieving effect, ritualizes everyday life and strengthens the children's will to survive. The brothers, however, feel cheated when it turns out that the letters were not sent at all, but a friend wisely explains to them: "Sometimes you don't tell the little ones the whole truth. You protect them, because the truth is complicated" (S02E04M32; own translation) – and what could be more complicated than the demise of modernity? They decide to send the letters anyway. The

Protect children from post-modern reality or introduce them in an age-appropriate way? Only order in everyday life and hope for the return of modernity will make them capable of living – at least surviving

youngest notices that the mailbox is emptied at 5:30 pm. Patiently and good-naturedly they explain: "You can't rely on that, Lukas. But that it will be emptied at some point, that's one hundred percent." (S02E04M38; own translation) Together they turn to God, as grandma would have done: they ask Him for an end to the pandemic – because ultimately writing a letter or an entry in the diary is nothing more than a modern form of prayer (cf. fig. 34). The fact that an early return to their accustomed order of life nevertheless remains unlikely weighs heavily on the two boys, which is why the children deserve the greatest attention and the strongest share of the remaining modern fragments.

All these methods of trying to cope with the transitional phase between modernity and post-modernity unfortunately do not help against the very practical everyday problems that such a life brings with it. Suddenly you have to do everything yourself: plant potatoes, dispose of dead animals from a barn, and defend yourself against the pirates (who appeared during the high phase as conspiracy preachers) who want to rob the island ("Well, for sure they're not from the national disaster control, they're badass motherfuckers" S02E06M23; own translation). Even simply looting the island and rummaging through the abandoned family homes for usable items is too strenuous for the young people, who are no longer accustomed to any particular hardships in the modern age. That's precisely why they fall so quickly for the temptation associated with the local drug dealer's power generator – but

Modern young people conceivably ill-prepared for post-modern life – no one has educated them to be independent

it's not free to recharge your useless cell phone there. Because there's nothing left to 'google', the pregnant Evelin realizes, looking from the island to the mainland: "If it's like here over there, if this is life now, then we're definitely the generation most ill-prepared for it." (S02E03M18; own translation) Perhaps it would not have been harmful to instill in young people, even and especially under modern conditions, a minimum of independence and a healthy basic skepticism about the unfulfillable promise of eternal availability of modern temptations. Without smartphones, a service society and helicopter parents, even the more grown-up children here are pretty much up the creek and survive only because they feed on the residual modernity – as long as there is still something of it left.

Figure 34: "Dear God, make sure that Mom and Dad are well and that the mailman comes soon to give them their letters. And that all the other people are well, too. And that the stupid pigeon flu is finally over. Amen." The children of Sløborn (S02E04M38; own translation) pray for a return of modernity, in which the community of the family replaces the loneliness of post-modernity.

Figure 35: Since a crass flu pandemic led to the apocalypse, including blackout, in Station Eleven *(S01E05M33), technological devices are only useless stuff. However, a group of survivors who managed to save themselves in a regional airport discover solar panels and rebuild their own little island of modern life.*

Is it possible to accept post-modernity as the new normal at some point, if you still knew modernity? And how do the first people born after the end of modernity fare? These questions are also at the center of the complex mini-series *Station Eleven* (USA 2022). Here, too, a globally raging virus wipes out almost all of humanity, with only about one percent of the species surviving. Jeevan, in a quarter-life crisis, survives the civilizational decline with little Kirsten only because he and his brother hid at home with a three-month supply shortly before the outbreak (see chapter 5). Even when a passenger plane crashes into an amusement park right before their eyes, the brother seems sure: "The way I see it, the power is on, everything will be back to normal in

Those who survive the transition to post-modernity find a world that has been written off – is it possible to settle here?

a couple of days." (S01E02M12) That they will not be right is shown by the time jumps of the series, which reach up to twenty years into the future: those who survived the pandemic Armageddon thanks to a face mask, satellite phone, total quarantine and a little luck (or misfortune?) must come to terms with the sudden unscheduled total write-off of modernity.

Two decades after the blackout, the modern world has vanished: the few surviving so-called "pre-pans" (those born before the pandemic) roam the woods in horse-drawn wagons; in a regional airport, the once stranded have built a commune complete with a solar cell on the roof and a "Museum of Civilization" with old technical stuff ("a tribute to the best of the old days, a reminder of how good we used to have it", S01E05M46; cf. fig. 35). For those born after the great dying (the "post-pans"), modernity is but a myth: when the now-adult Kirsten explains how smartphones could once be used to order cars to take you anywhere, and that they could talk to every nook and cranny in the world, it has the feel of an improbable but incredibly exciting miracle narrative for the young people of this post-modern world. Even the idea that most of humanity was once invisibly networked via wireless data link seems crazy ("So the internet was real then? ... Sounds beautiful", S01E06M41). Against this background, it is invaluable that some children had the presence of mind to quickly download Wikipedia onto their devices shortly before the collapse of modernity and thus of the power supply

Technologies of modernity seem like miracles to children born in the post-modern era – because hardly anything could be saved

and the Internet: with this copy of the world's largest encyclopedia, they have a last remnant of modern knowledge, which would otherwise have been long lost in this shut-down decayed world.

Just like little Kirsten, one of these children was given a graphic novel as a gift shortly before the start of the pandemic: a thin booklet entitled *Station Eleven*. The comic, of which only a few copies exist, tells the story of the lonely astronaut Dr. Eleven, who has to watch powerlessly as the world falls apart around him. While their own normality dies with the onset of the pandemic, the astonishingly apocalyptic and at the same time thoughtful children's book gives emotional support to the youngest and offers identification figures, because Dr. Eleven is still a child himself, lost and hopeless ("You're going to die and I can't stop it." S01E07M39; cf. fig. 36). While Kirsten still thinks of the story as an adult when she needs strength to continue her life in the post-modern era, Tyler (who compulsively devoured the comic during a month-long quarantine) gathers around him an army of "post-pan" children to whom he tells the story of Dr. Eleven so many times around the campfire until they believe it to be the truth – they *believe* in it. For the innocent, the stories of the sacrificing Dr. Eleven are a prophecy, Tyler for them "the Prophet" himself. The disoriented youngsters, who grow up without literature, film and television, without music and art, absorb everything that could give them meaning in their hopeless situation – and are easily instru-

Post-modernity produces new dangerous beliefs in myths and prophecies to which children are most easily victimized

mentalized for a senseless fight against the last remnants of modernity: the desolate Tyler wants to destroy the "Museum of Civilization", because in his memory the last days of modernity are associated only with failure, suffering and devastation, while life in post-modernity is associated with unexpected freedom. Again and again, the two quote a saying from the graphic novel that becomes a leitmotif for the transition to the post-modern world: "I don't want to live the wrong life and die" – they must learn to live right after modernity: "There is a before. It was just awful. I release you from the Undersea." (S01E08M50)

Only when Kirsten shows the children, who have been abused as suicide bombers, that their myth is nothing more than a comic book and that their beloved prophet is only an adult who has remained a wounded lonely child at heart, they have a chance to overcome their misbelief and can drop their hatred of modernity. The problem, however, that this world also needs some form of social standardization and binding values remains unsolved with the overcoming of these neo-religious practices. Post-modernity will have to acquire new methods to integrate the lives of "pre-pans" and "post-pans" alike, those born before and those born after the onset of post-modernity – otherwise the lack of meaning leads to a collapse within the collapse.

> Disenchantment of myths diminishes hatred of past modernity – but also leaves gap in meaning making

Figure 36: "... I was just lonely. This strange and awful time was the happiest of my life. You're the only friend I've ever had." (S01E07M39) Little Kirsten finds with Station Eleven *an allegory for her own (post-)pandemic abandonment in the multilayered tale of the lonely Dr. Eleven and his mentor Dr. Logan. In the moment of greatest loneliness, the astronaut figure appears to her as a bodily counterpart, just as it once did to the author herself. (S01E04M29)*

In most post-apocalyptic series about life in the de-electrified post-modern world, a trigger is needed that indirectly causes the blackout and thus leads to the downfall of the accustomed techno-civilization. Strikingly, however, among all the pandemic, zombie and other horror stories, there are also narratives in which electrification *itself* directly leads to its downfall. The series *Revolution* (USA 2012–2014), canceled after two seasons, is not about a sudden positive social disruption, as the title suggests, but about a reversal of evolution, or one could say: a *remodernization*. One evening, all electronic devices worldwide deactivate: cars stop, airplanes crash, cell phones and computers are off –

Out-of-control techno-modernism destroys itself

(almost) forever. The core story of the series takes place 15 years after the great blackout: "We lived in an electric world. We relied on it for everything. And then the power went out. Everything stopped working. We weren't prepared. Fear and confusion lead to panic. [...] We still don't know why the power went out, but we're hopeful that someone will come and light the way," says a recap at the beginning of each episode (see fig. 37). But the way points only in the direction of the deconstruction of modernity: North America has disintegrated into six 'republics', which fight each other in (lengthy) slaughters and fight for supremacy in a rather dull auxiliary feudalism. The world sinks into a de-industrialized, de-electrified, and thus demodernized 'pre-history' in which children die of polio again: "This is the world we live in now." (S02E01M20; own translation) As the series progresses, it gradually emerges where the cause of the blackout originated: dedicated scientists were working on a solution to the global energy problem just before the big shutdown. They thought that they found a technology to produce cheap electricity. The developed nanorobots, however, caused exactly the opposite of what was hoped for: the invention did not produce electricity, but localized mini-blackouts, as the particles absorb the electricity from their surroundings. Of course, only the Ministry of Defense could be enthusiastic about such a destructive accidental invention, even though the risk of misuse and accidental activation is more than obvious.

Figure 37: 15 years after the blackout, nature has reclaimed most of the world in Revolution *(S01E01M05). Humanity needs to make peace with these new post-modern conditions – but instead they are warring for dominance over the newly divided US.*

The head of the bankrupt research group sells the idea to the military, even though his pregnant wife advises him against it; after all, their research results, which were developed out of honorable impulse, could be used as a weapon against humanity. Eventually, the nanobots spread all over the world: "Each one is the size of a virus. They are everywhere. They're in the air, on buildings, and we're breathing them in right now," she later explains amid a degenerate world which has had its power sucked out by the minicomputers: "We had destroyed the world." (S01E13M07; own translations) A decade and a half after the great blackout, control over the last traces of electricity determines

Domination over remnants of electrified modernity decisive in post-modernity over distribution of political power winners and losers in the War of the New Republics. This ongoing struggle for power in the post-modern era becomes the plot-driving theme of the series, as a few have a flash drive that locally neutralizes the effect and contains the solution to the problem – but those who benefited from the blackout show no interest in turning the lights back on.

At the end of the first season, the characters realize that a reactivation of modernity would be quite possible by reprogramming the nano computers, which are bent on destruction, multiplying uncontrollably. Whether this is a good idea after 15 years without electricity, however, remains a controversial question: in the season finale (S01E20), it becomes apparent that the global power outage was deliberately induced at the time and that the same backdoor in the code can now be used to reverse the global blackout. When the world is turned back on, the Earth is covered with huge thunderbolts, but for a few minutes it seems to work: lights come on, radios buzz again – and, unfortunately, so do the hatches of the silos of several nuclear missiles fired by a madman at two major cities to take out two recalcitrant republics and thus 'unite the nation' (cf. fig. 38). The re-engagement proves to be a double-edged sword, but it also only lasts for a few minutes. At the beginning of the second season, the world is already in darkness again and one is annoyed with increasing mysterious phenomena, which were obviously triggered by the brief reactivation of the power. In a four-part comic series that replaces the

Re-engaging the modern age succeeds only in the short term – but leaves more harm than good behind

unrealized third season, it turns out that the nano-technology can be used not only to create energy blackouts, but also to control behavior and produce hallucinations in humans. It's no surprise that by the end of the story here, people are fed up with electricity: in a post-modern world, all in all, electricity will not do any good. In the long run, one will have to come to terms with the fact that electricity is not coming back.

Figure 38: After 15 years of powerlessness, at the end of the first season of Revolution *(S01E20M38), the great rewiring succeeds, if only for four minutes. Unfortunately, the short time is enough to send off atomic bombs that had been useless in their missile silos since the global blackout.*

In a certain sense, then, *Tribes of Europa* (D 2021) can be read like a continuation of the plot of *Revolution*. The plot takes place in the year 2074, almost half a century after the devastating "Black December": since a global blackout in 2029, the

Modern world without electricity disintegrates into hodgepodge of retrograde, dictatorial tribes

world has gradually reverted to primitive tribal structures that fight each other. While only the so-called "Atlantians" are known to have survived the collapse of the technological age, Europe consists only of the titular tribes: the Origines live in a kind of retarded eco-communism in the forests; the fascistic Crows run a slave factory for the ominous "Wolk" resource in their capital Brahtok (formerly "Berlin"), which they use to finance their grotesque initiation rituals and perverse humiliation fantasies; the militaristic Crimson Republic emerged from the former 'Eurocorps' and pretends to protect the other tribes; and then there is the Flemish Union (disbanded "they captured our monarch and decapitated him", S01E03M10), the Basque Country, the Southern Regions, the Red Legions and of course the Northern Alliance (Scandinavia is still comfortable – even in the post-modern era)... New languages have emerged in crumbling Europe, mostly convoluted mixtures of earlier modern lingua francas, signaling: a lot of time has passed here, and everything has changed since the death of modernity. Without electricity, civilization is doomed, and the only choice is between an exhausting pre-modern life among the bushes or membership in some terrorist, dictatorial or fragile pseudo-state. It is almost a good thing that hardly anyone here remembers the modern era, because the sense of how well one could do there would probably be too painful in the long run.

Young Elja of the Origines, on the other hand, is interested in nothing more than the life of the past – and above all: why it ended. Before her death, his mother had created a mausoleum of times past in a hiding place: on the walls hang old newspaper articles with headlines à la "Frexit", "Cyberwar" and "EU declares state of emergency". In front of them are old smartphones, game consoles and bicycle lamps, which of course no longer work, but prove that modernity must have existed (S01E01M18). When an Atlantian crashes over the settlement of the Origines, Elja has contact with working electronics for the first time, and even with a particularly advanced one, for which people in Europe are willing to kill: the injured pilot reports that the mysterious (unfortunately defective) metal cube warns of an imminent danger coming from the east towards Europe – now only the people of the "Lost Ark" know what to do. Elja takes the Cube and meets the opportunistic but good-natured Moses, who helps him get the device working again: it projects an animation of the approaching danger. Moses wants to sell the device and (in addition to visits to brothels in the Northern Alliance) use it to finance himself and Elja's petrol for life – but in fact the Cube is destined for greater things, because it shows the way out of the impending catastrophe and is therefore invaluable.

Remnants of functioning electronics become holy relics in post-modernity

The odd guy with a narrow mustache steers a modified Volkswagen LT45 4x4 (it also runs without a computer), on which the electronic scrap dealer (a profitable profession in these times) has shuttered fuel canisters, a solar panel and other useful things for life in the post-modern age. On their road trip to Italian music from the 2010s, they puzzle together over what might have once triggered the blackout, the "Black December". The teenage Elja speculates: "Was it to do with the cyberattacks between the old superpowers? Or was it a military super-virus?" (S01E03M01) The oddball bon vivant in his fifties has witnessed the collapse of the modern world himself on December 31, 2029: "All transportation, by water, by land, by air: bosh, off! The Internet, mobile phones: bosh! Tablets, computers – lights off and darkness. And that was that. Middle Ages." (S01E03M02) – But even he doesn't know the causes of the downfall. Nevertheless, it is certain for him: the Atlantians could have survived the blackout as the only "Tribe" only because they were prepared – either because they would have caused the blow against the modern world themselves, or because they simply knew what was coming and have taken precautions. Europe, on the other hand, has been thrown back into the 16th century by the blackout. The answer to how this could have happened is likely to move not only the characters (who are driven primarily by curiosity), but also the clueless audience (who, after all, live in the modern age, and thus are likely to still face the blackout somewhen in their own reality). The characters in

How did the devastating blackout happen? Only the originators or the prepared could survive collapse

256

this series sacrifice everything for a chance to find part of the answer, why the blackout happened.

This is not surprising, because the techno-remnants from the past radiate a magical aura over them. Moses, for example, has found an old can and wants to try out his still functioning Tandoo opener (see fig. 39). They smile in fascination, perhaps moved by how the small blue plastic part cuts open the metal. What do you think modernity was capable of, and what else could it have achieved, if such things had once existed? The fact that the can has been expired for 44 years doesn't bother Moses: "The best-before date was an invention of the food manufacturing industry" – but unfortunately the beans didn't survive that long. The very idea, however, that there used to be ready-to-eat foods packed in a can creates a mixture of fetish and disbelief. There is little justified hope of reclaiming modernity here: people are content to preserve what they have, and that's not much. The young people, however, for whom life in the bushes, in the forced camp of the fascists, or in the military state is not enough, feel the urge for change, but they do not know in which direction to channel it, and there is no other place beyond this anti-modernity to which they could take refuge.

Fascination of the electrical devices of the past, which are fossils reminiscent of better times – that will not come back

Figure 39: To open the can from modern times, you wouldn't need the electric helper – but in the de-electrified post-modernity of Tribes of Europa *(S01E03M11), every functioning technical device seems like a miracle.*

Therefore, the setting does not really differ from the conditions in the successful German mystery series *Dark* (D 2017–2020). The young people in particular feel as if they are locked up in the eerie village of Winden: on the one hand the small town is on the drip of the prosperous nuclear power plant, and on the other hand its inhabitants feel that the reactor must have something to do with the strange things that have been happening here for 66 years. Rarely has a series title anticipated so much what will happen in the episodes: in Winden it is always *dark*, even during the day, it rains constantly, otherwise it is cloudy, it is gray and bleak, it's just uneasy all the time. The highly complex (and a bit stretched) time travel narrative plays out philosophical concepts of causal relationships between

Power failure triggers mysterious processes – laws of nature seem to act up

past, present and future, where – as one never tires of repeating here – somehow 'everything is connected'. The series debuts with a suicide on a rope – and a power outage, again: first, only the milk is sour and the toaster doesn't work, but later a child disappears without a trace (as we will learn later, into the past). Through a chain of different circumstances, time travel is possible in Winden, which makes life in the small town even more complicated than it already is in such a small German town, and dissolves the logical relations of an idea of time as a linear course.

In 2020, at any rate, a fatal mix of nuclear industry cover-up of an incident, wormholes, and out-of-control elementary particles brings about the eagerly awaited apocalypse: a mysterious matter in the nuclear power plant swallows up Winden. The main hero, Jonas, a high school student, lands shortly before in a post-modern world 33 years after his own present and realizes that the disaster at the power plant has left his loved ones dead and the world itself out of balance. Apparently, for a nanosecond, the end-time event at Winden had caused a global blackout that threw the world into chaos: for an instant, time literally ended. The young man begins an energy-sapping round trip through the history of modernization in the hope of changing the past in such a way that it does not come to the doom – although of course in the meantime, as it also belongs to time travel narratives, everything gets worse and worse and the end of the world, which leads to the deelectrified age, cannot be stopped at first, on the

Power outage as a sign of the uncanny and the unmanageable – post-modernity escalates experience of loneliness

contrary: the world splits into several parallel universes, making everything even more confusing – and uninfluenceable. In general, the overall situation is opaque for everyone involved, but one thing is certain: whenever the light flickers and the next blackout announces itself, the characters know that something sinister, uncontrollable, inevitable is about to happen again. The characters' experiences of loneliness escalate, as they feel defenseless against the uncontrollable events in their living world: every attempt to eliminate the chaos leads deeper and deeper into a post-historical end time.

It is not until the third season that Jonas realizes that he must prevent an all-decisive moment of fate in one of the parallel worlds in order to stop the apocalypse of Winden and thus the death of the people he loves. If there had not been the tragic accidental death of his family, the clockmaker and time machine manufacturer Tannhaus would have had no interest in intervening in the dense fabric of history and its inscrutable causal structures. With his desperate attempt to change the tragic course of events, he had evidently upset everything in the first place. When Jonas encounters a shadow of his beloved Martha in this parallel world, they give the watchmaker's relatives a good scare, lest they drive through the dark night in the rain. In a last scene in the series finale ("Paradise", cf. fig. 40) reminiscent of the haunting imagery of Gregory Crewdson, Jonas and Martha wonder what will happen to them when their plan succeeds and their illusory worlds

Figures sacrifice everything to prevent the blackout and thus the onset of post-modernity

produced by the blackout no longer exist: "I wonder if anything of us will remain. Or is that what we
are? A dream? That we never really existed?"
(S03E08M59) The struggle to avert the global
blackout in the future reality has cost them everything – not only their lives, but even the memory of
them and even the certainty of whether they ever
really lived at all. Since the small family obviously
arrives back home safely, the end of the world in
2020 is thus averted – but with it, Jonas and Martha's eternal loneliness is also perfect.

The series ends in the modern electrified present – with a power outage, of course. As the characters sit in the dark at a plentiful dinner, the impression is that the hidden events have taken root in
them, leaving a trail of longing for post-modernity.
One character recalls her nighttime dream that anticipated the final blackout: "It was just dark and it
was never light again. And the weird thing is that it
felt really good. For everything to be over. Like suddenly being free of everything. No wants. No needs.
Unending darkness. No yesterday. No today. No tomorrow. Nothing." (S03E08M68) Perhaps there really is something liberating about a post-modernity
that can be observed from a protected distance,
without actually having to enter it and be exposed
to its dangers – like a movie or TV series that tells
of the blackout and the end of electrified modernity,
without us actually having to live through all that.
Perhaps only in the sight of this dark post-modernity does the real world of the present appear in the
right light: a modernity that is worth preserving.

Longing for the
blackout as a sign
of collective fear of
post-modernity

Figure 40: In Dark *(S02E08M63), the end of modernity in the form of the blackout apocalypse can only be stopped by elaborate journeys through time and well-calculated interventions in the course of events. The main characters sacrifice their lives together for the preservation of modern life: the price for averting post-modernity is their happiness – and the memory that they ever existed.*

9. MODERNITY MUST GO ON: THE COMEDY OF THE BLACKOUT

In the TV series and feature films presented up to this point, power failures that push society to the edge of its resilience and blackouts that call civilization as a whole into question are regularly a burden for the characters, who have to deal with and adjust to the consequences. Clearly limited power failures, however, whose effects remain controllable and whose imminent end is foreseeable beyond doubt, pose no real danger – and can sometimes even be fun. Because such situations temporarily pause the usual normality of life to a non-threatening degree, they lend themselves perfectly to comedic forms of entertainment, placing a challenging but harmless glitch in the otherwise lighthearted cosmos of film and television characters that will be fixed in time for the end of the evening or episode sequence. In the meantime, the incident provides an opportunity to make visible the interdependent relationships between people that are otherwise hidden in the anonymous service society, driving the characters to reflect on (and possibly even renew) their social relationships with one another and become more resilient in the process. Even if the characters initially react fearfully and they sometimes even panic, they have the chance in the end – as long as the return to modernity remains possible – to grow closer together and emerge stronger from the experience of crisis.

As long as consequences of the blackout remain manageable, it can give even pleasure and initiate reflection of social relations

Power outages, like burglaries, births in unusual places or storms, are standard situations in any sitcom, and the only time they're missing from a series is when the show is just canceled too soon. The teens from H_2O: *Just Add Water* (AU 2006–2010), for instance, who moonlight as bona fide mermaids, accidentally cause a domestic energy crisis with their magic crystals, causing their father to miss the outcome of the big soccer game on TV (S03E21). *Malcolm in the Middle* (USA 2000–2006) has secretly three Dutch girls at home, but after an evening full of confusion and a power outage, little Dewey (otherwise the weakest link in the food chain) manages to bag the trio for himself (S07E07). In the *Cosby's* house (USA 1996–2000), the family prepares for the millennium bug on New Year's Eve 1999, but the generator, of all things, which is supposed to safeguard the bourgeois life in the event of the 'end of the world', causes the blackout in the neighborhood (S04E06, "Lucas Apocalypse"). But the neighborhood knows how to help itself: to calm the tempers, hamburgers are grilled on the street and cupcakes are baked, and even though supplies for the end times are quickly depleted, the spontaneous feast results in love at first sight, at least for Griffin. Iconic pleb Al Bundy is *Married... With Children* (USA 1987–1997) and to take care of his awkward white-trash clan: during a heat wave, he acquires from ominous sources an old German air conditioner still set to "blitzkrieg". Since it needs heavy current, he simply taps into the public power line, causing a blackout throughout the district that escalates into

> Power outages as minor disruptions to otherwise carefree sitcom reality create easily resolved mini-conflicts

a lynch mob within ten seconds. Because there's never any real danger in the sitcom world, the characters only have to wonder how the neighbors got their pitchforks so quickly. Fortunately, Al has a plan B and puts his pack, which is experienced in scrounging, in the local supermarket next to the freezers – because a blackout in such a temple of consumption would certainly not be expected of the American sitcom audience and thus also of the TV family. German Comedian *Pastewka* (D 2005–2014, 2018–2020), for example, has to spend the episode "Das Gewitter" ("The Thunderstorm", S05E08) with his neighbor against their will. The lady, with whom he has a love-hate relationship typical of the genre, refuses to be shaken off and calls for neighborly help when the power goes out ("Do you have a fucking candle for me? Yes or no?" S05E08M04; own translation). Because colleague and buddy Opdenhövel, a showmaster from German television, doesn't know how to help either, they pass the time with a spontaneous (analog) round of "Schlag den Star", which he normally chairs on TV. And Felix from the law firm *Edel und Starck* (D 2002–2005) is entirely responsible for the power outage he causes in the office – the general overhaul of the power lines, brimming with masculinity, on the other hand, makes him only more desirable in the eyes of his colleague Rebecca (S03E01)...

The comical sitcom power outages leave no doubt that the modern age can put away an exceptional situation like the surprising stillstand of electricity: the affected characters behave in such a way

Darkness helps with secrecy, but power outage can blow their cover that, all things considered, carefree modern life can continue as usual at the end of the episode. Nonetheless, the mini-blackouts can really shake up the habits typical of such series, so that new storylines emerge. The *Desperate Housewives* (USA 2004–2012) are known for their diverse, otherwise well-kept secrets. But when the power goes out in suburban Fairview, it's not just "a minor inconvenience" (S03E19M01), but a curse and a blessing at the same time. Blessing is for those who want to organize feeding orgies under the cover of darkness, browse through father's men's magazines unobserved, or use the opportunity for seduction – that is, to keep and further develop their secrets. The characters also find the danger of being caught by the firemen during a spontaneous intimate moment in the elevator obviously arousing. The blackout, on the other hand, is a curse for those who have a frozen husband lying in their basement. The odd but kind-hearted Karen McCluskey has stored her husband in the freezer after his passing so that she can continue to draw his pension. When she misses a step during the power outage and tumbles down the stairs, there's no way she wants to go to the hospital – because of the irreplaceable frozen 'food' with 'lovers' value' that she has yet to get ice for. When the power comes back on, she lulls herself into safety, but a short circuit threatens to expose her secret. Ultimately, however, each of these secrets, even with old McCluskey, is fraught with inconvenience in the event of exposure – but no one really has anything to fear here. Modern life for all involved will simply go on the next day as if nothing had happened.

Sometimes the consequences of the blackout are quite chaotic, even in comedic series. The police department *Brooklyn Nine-Nine* (USA 2013–) has enough problems to deal with (which they often cause themselves and then have to pay for). When the power goes out in the neighborhood, romantic feelings rise in the infantile but smart Detective Jake: "You know, I've always kind of liked blackouts. Listen to how quiet it is. It's so peaceful" – But when, after just a few seconds of darkness, the first shots ring out, "it immediately turned into a purge. Way to go, New York!" Because the phones aren't working, everything seems fine at first, but who's going to call without service? Smart-ass Jake gets to philosophizing: "Huh, really makes you think about society's reliance on modern technology, doesn't it?" (S07E13M02) The officials set the right priorities and first turn their attention to the perishable supplies in the refrigerator, which must be rescued (in other words: eaten up) as quickly as possible (cf. fig. 41). The claustrophobic police chief can fortunately distract himself from his fear in the stuck elevator with cool dance moves, while his heavily pregnant deputy continues to work even after her water has broken ("My water just broke, which reminds me: we should be prepared to distribute emergency water and food", S03E13M06). While Jake, the father, gallops to the station on horseback with no riding experience, the two insatiable, otherwise quite useless police officers have improvised

Power outage underlines the already chaotic conditions visible at the moment of crisis

a birthing room: "We've been napping at work for 20 years. We know how to create a relaxing space in a police station: gurney, fire blankets, night stick for back massages, soothing lights – aka Scully's fart candles" (S07E13M16). In the meantime, even bank robbers can be caught, and public order remains unscathed apart from some traffic jams and unauthorized urination into a trash can. All in all, the impression here is that the blackout makes no real difference, because at the end of this adventure everything will be the same as before – with the difference that there is one more Earth citizen.

Figure 41: Known for their ravenous appetites, their colleagues from the Brooklyn Nine-Nine *police department (S07E13M06) have made it their heroic mission to save the refrigerated products from spoilage during the blackout. Fortunately, when things get serious, they do make themselves useful.*

Unfortunately, *The Simpsons* (USA 1989–) are not that lucky. Again, it's a season finale (S13E22) that launches the world's yellowest family into its summer break. During a fierce heat wave, all the air conditioners in Springfield are running at full blast, morgues are used for resting, everything is sweating and burning. Even the school is suddenly attractive, because there is an AC that is about to go berserk. Although electricity is to be saved, all the lights in the Simpsons' house are on anyway, of course – only they don't have air conditioning. Homer hopes for cooling in the sight of an electric dancing Santa Claus toy figure – but it is exactly this one watt that brings the barrel to overflow, prompting the city-wide blackout. Even the shutdown of the orphanage ("Who are they going to complain to? Their parents?" S13E22M03) can't prevent the overload of the nuclear power plant. The senseless looting begins directly, to which the middle class citizens are rather carried away out of boredom. Some even simply rob themselves, stealing stones or burning tires from the municipal garbage dump. Because the police don't prove to be very helpful, Homer sets up his own private security company, which is entrusted with exercising the monopoly on violence in the city. The chaos in the city – even after the blackout – will not decrease as a result.

Power outage draws attention to dysfunctional social structures and institutions

Sometimes, however, unexpected chaos also brings surprising positive changes. In the feature film *Yesterday* (UK 2019), a brief global blackout has surprising consequences: the entire world's pop-

Short power outage as a trigger for social and individual change

ulation – with the exception of a lucky few, including unsuccessful wannabe rock star Jack – suddenly can't remember the Beatles' songs. After the Eiffel Tower, the Berlin Gate and the Kremlin, as well as stores, stadiums and news channels, were without power for exactly twelve seconds, the collective memory of the most successful band in pop history seems to have been erased. While the world puzzles over how the belated "Millennium Bug" came about (newspapers speculate about solar storms), Jack forces himself to remember the melodies (that's easy) and the lyrics (that's hard) – and becomes so quickly so successful with 'his' new songs that Ed Sheeran with his comparatively naïve songs can only stand pale beside them. The blackout swirls the world here in a strange way, because at first glance, not much has changed – and yet, "a world without the Beatles is a world that's infinitely worse." (M91) After Jack's life is turned around into an unprecedented success story, he meets an unsuspecting John Lennon in an idyllic beach house, who didn't write any songs but had a full life. In some mysterious way, the blackout has apparently rewritten entire biographies, intervened in the innermost fabric of the world and discreetly shaken it up – but ultimately not for the worse, because in the end Jack makes the appropriated songs available for free download and finally finds his eternal love from youth. And the fact that the world apparently can't remember "Harry Potter" either is not noticed by anyone at all and accordingly doesn't seem to bother anyone – the blackout takes and the blackout gives.

Figure 42: "You call that a glowstick? That is a glow stick!" – Leonard senses that there is no danger from the power failure in the apartment building, because outside everything is brightly lit and the janitor will take care of it in a moment. Rather, the mini-blackout staged by Sheldon produces (thanks to darkness and wine) new opportunities for a rapprochement with Penny (The Big Bang Theory, *S05E15M13).*

If a blackout can really mess things up in a comedy series, it's in the well-ordered world of *The Big Bang Theory*, because the brilliant astrophysicist Dr. Sheldon Cooper suffers from obsessive-compulsive behavior, as a result of which his entire life is determined by routines and rules. His comparatively harmless roommate Leonard occasionally gets caught up in the mills of neurotic tics. Every quarter, for example, a disaster preparedness exercise is scheduled, in which the flatmates' resilience against typical apocalyptic crisis scenarios ("everything from wild fires to a surprise invasion by Canada"

Power outage allows clarification of conflicts and social relations

S05E15M01) is tested and trained at random. After the two have to spend another sleepless night "dressed like one of the Village People" (S05E15M02), Leonard cancels the "Roommate Agreement", which clarifies in amazing detail his (few) rights and (many) duties to Sheldon. The pedantic boy in a man's body, who is not at all capable of a life without outside help, tries to lure Leonard back into the roommate agreement with an artifice. He stages a power failure in the apartment block with a small intervention in the fuse box of the house in order to show Leonard his extensive emergency equipment, which he naturally keeps on hand for such cases: glow-in-the-dark lights (he removed his carcinogenic photoluminescent escape signs), a "deep-cycle marine battery power source more than capable of running our entertainment system" (M14), matching DVDs, snacks, a Bunsen burner, and a reverse osmosis machine ("It took me a gallon of urine to make that water", M17; cf. fig. 42). Penny, on the other hand, has only candles (which, according to Sheldon, are a fire hazard!), wine, plenty of bubble wrap (to tide over the boredom) – and, of course, herself: "Anyway, you wanna make out? [...] Lucky for you there's nothing else to do right now." (M15) Sheldon underestimates the power of the romantic mix of candlelight, darkness, and distraction that effectively distracts Leonard from his fiction of the world ending without electricity. Under such conditions, nothing seems to matter now, because according to Sheldon, the blackout means anarchy: "The world has descended into darkened turmoil. Lawlessness and savagery are the order of the day." (M16) The fact that the lights are on in the neighboring houses as if nothing had happened has to be imagined away. Penny, with her special emotional intelligence, recognizes that Sheldon's core concern is not the roommate agreement, but the loneliness he experiences without his friendship with Leonard ("I think he misses his little buddy", M16). Although the blackout was artificially induced, it serves as an occasion to release years of frustration full with lack of gratitude and to make a new agreement that will make life better. But it wouldn't be a sitcom if almost everything wasn't back to normal in the next episode.

In general, the comical blackouts in TV series are always the moments when previously anonymous neighborhoods and strangers can get to know each other anew and get together, especially in the modern big city, where people otherwise just live past each other. Of course, the unforgettable *Friends* (USA 1994–2004) have each other after all, but the blackout becomes an occasion to redefine the complex social relations (S01E07). The boredom of the blackout unearths some surprising intimate secrets that only further solidify the bonds of friendship. Will Ross take the opportunity to finally confess his feelings to the adored Rachel (Jennifer Aniston) under the light of Hanukkah candles to still avoid imprisonment in the dreaded "friendship zone"? As he gathers his courage, the deep romantic conversation is interrupted by a stray cat. In search of the owner, they encounter some creepy oddball

Power outage as an occasion for initiating romantic partnerships in the neighborhood, but also just the attractive Italian who doesn't speak a word of English, but successfully sweet-talks the languishing Rachel with his long black hair. Obviously, power outages set a considerable pace in romantic terms, which is not compatible with the hesitant mating procedures typical for the modern era. Chandler, on the other hand, would actually have ideal conditions for turning his situation into a chance at mating: he is locked in the vestibule of a bank branch – together with a "Victoria's Secret" model. The dapper blonde initially makes a rather bored, but also not really averse impression – but Chandler manages to increasingly unsettle the lady with his grotesque behavior until she feels visibly uncomfortable. Only when the underwear model saves his life rather casually (he has choked on chewing gum and she uses the Heimlich maneuver – inevitable in sitcoms), the distance gradually diminishes and the further hours together in the store even become quite fun. In the modern age, it's apparently possible to live quite well, even if the power is out for a few hours.

Time and again, sitcoms need the power outage to bring the characters back to the fact that their everyday problems don't matter in the grand scheme of things. In the terribly innocuous world of *Growing Pains* (USA 1985–1992), the penultimate episode of the series (S07E22) once again neatly upsets the lives of the Seaver family: they get stuck in a traffic jam, can't escape the bad food of a medieval banquet, and have to calm down their young daughter, who is afraid of the dark. In the end, the parents

During blackout, sufferers suddenly rediscover missing communities use the time in the traffic jam to get closer to each other again after a long time, they pull out the guitar to sing a song and also stay cuddled together in the armchair when the electricity is back: "I like it here with you." (M23)

Figure 43: Steve Urkel tries to create a Christmas atmosphere in a stopped Metro train. The grouchy city dwellers take out their anger on him, which is actually pointed against their own living situation. However, the memory of the small miracles of modern everyday life makes them forget the blackout. (Family Matters, S05E11M16)

Even in the Winslow house, where *Family Matters* (USA 1989–1998) and for the genre also unusually socially critical themes are struck, no real Christmas feeling (S05E11) wants to arise when Carl is stuck in the subway with Steve Urkel, the

Blackout interrupts dysfunctional daily routines and brings people together – for a short moment

weird but smart and kind-hearted neighbor's son. The tired and hungry people on the stuck train are fed up with their daily routine and unsatisfying jobs – the blackout is the last thing they need. The somewhat defiant but good-natured Steve tries to lift the mood in the wagon through games, songs and jokes (cf. fig. 43), but reaps only dislike, insults and hatred. Steve's pushiness becomes a catalyst for the general discontent of modern city dwellers, who prefer to mope around in a bad mood – and yet, through a few upright words, he manages to appeal to a sense of community in the midst of the blackout: in anticipation of the happiness waiting on Christmas Eve, they decorate a makeshift Christmas tree together and forget about their deplorable situation.

Maybe sometimes it takes an occasion to break up stuck thoughts, let go of inherently irrelevant everyday problems and sort out childish conflicts. In the meta-universe of the self-reflective *High School Musical – The Musical – The Series* (USA 2019–), the youngsters drag a whole lot of 'first world problems' through the hallways of mythical-iconic *East High*, most of which they eat into themselves: creative stage diva Gina feels she and her dance ideas are being shortchanged by head choreographer Carlos, songstress Nini has always dreamed of studying at the elite drama high school but is terribly lonely there, and pretty sportsman E. J. feels his parents' pressure to succeed. It takes a moment of honesty in the middle of the second season, organized by the citywide blackout: because of a storm (S02E04), the

Modern everyday problems fade in the moment of the power blackout, which at the same time offers a chance for rethinking

members of the theater group are snowed in at their powerless school along with their guidance counselor, and Nini is stuck in a car with the head of the musical study group. During the crisis, they suddenly can't avoid each other and hide in the suburban mansions that are far too big, and the problems they had previously repressed and smiled away come up: Gina and Carlos realize that they are not fighting each other at all, but their modern identity crises (homosexuality and hypermobility), E. J. senses in conversation with the gifted computer science teacher that he has a right to shape his own life dreams despite his success biography, and Nini understands that great goals can change once you've looked them in the eye. In the Disney universe, everyone is always pretty sweet to each other anyway, but after the big talk, even the last potential for conflict seems temporarily exhausted – and the carefree life of prosperity can continue. Nevertheless, the small adventure also appears as a dangerous exceptional situation. Gina uses the crises to show her leadership skills: "Rehearsal can wait. Follow my lead. Contact your parents every half hour, but conserve your phone batteries. Waters, flashlights. Let's move, people!" (M12) The brief moment of danger in an inherently harmless situation unleashes self-protective forces in young people inexperienced with disasters that could be useful during a real blackout. But the longing for modern normality sets in surprisingly quickly: after just one hour without food or smartphone, the order for emergency cannibalism is already being clarified and a power bank is being fought over. Fortunately, a brave pizza delivery boy has already wrestled his way through the snowstorm to the famished, and at that moment the electricity also returns – and with it a whole series of important life decisions: a return to community, which is embedded in the myth of *High School Musical* and its characters and can easily be buried under the lonely mechanisms of modernization.

Perhaps the greatest blessing of the television blackout is that it brings a modern society – otherwise spoiled by the constant availability of consumer things and services – somewhat into perspective: in view of the injustices and errors that continue to exist, as well as the successes achieved and the constantly emerging miracles of modern society, its inhabitants are allowed to ask themselves from time to time whether, in the midst of an escalating climate catastrophe – driven by wasteful consumption, immoderate meat consumption and a reckless throwaway mentality – the standards have not become confused. In the *Superstore* (USA 2015–2021), for example, just about everything that modern consumer society has to offer for consumption can be found under one roof. It's not until a tornado (S02E22) causes a power outage, blows the roof off the store and devastates the shop worse than a "Black Friday", that the employees realize amid the ruins of the full-range store what a wonder world they actually live in (cf. fig. 44): "When you think about it, a store like this is actually pretty incredible," Jonah concludes at the end of the series –

Only in the face of the blackout does the real value of modernity become apparent brightly lit by the soft supermarket light, accompanied by the whir of air conditioners, surrounded by endless consumer goods on sale (S06E15M17).

But modernity is more than consumption, waste and kitsch. It is the place we have created for our lives and without which we can now no longer live. Modernity, however, is above all an idea: hope for a humanity that is never conclusively fixed, where relationships, roles, and dreams can change, where we can *modernize,* without everything becoming arbitrary. Like the hopeless characters, we would only really miss it if we were to lose it. The blackout films and series speak a common language: an end to modernity is the last thing that should happen to us.

Figure 44: In disbelief, the employees of the Superstore *(S02E22M20) look at the devastation wrought by the tornado. What modernity has to offer can only really be seen when it eludes us.*

THE CHECKLIST:
WHAT YOU SHOULD HAVE
AT HOME

We live in times of high supply security, and we can be grateful for that. Even longer power outages or supply shortages are familiar to most of us (if not from movies and television) at most from the stories of our great-grandparents. Nevertheless, you can be temporarily on your own because of a blackout, for example. So that you can then help yourself as best you can, I have compiled the most important "lessons" from the films and shows examined for you in this checklist. Have you thought of everything to be well prepared in the event of an emergency?

For the most part, the checklist also corresponds to the official recommendations for emergency preparedness for power outages of the German Federal Office of Civil Protection and Disaster Assistance (BBK) and, like film and television, goes beyond them in places. Nevertheless, the listing should be understood as a rough guide only. It is no substitute for thinking for yourself and planning your own precautionary requirements realistically. For official guidance on topics such as emergency stockpiling and preparing for other crisis situations such as extreme weather events and pandemics, please visit the BBK website at *bbk.bund.de/EN* or get more detailed information from your local disaster control authority like the Federal Emergency Management Agency (FEMA) in the US.

❑ So that you don't have to fight with your fellow citizens over a bottle of mineral water like in *Awake* or *Then There Was,* you should have **30 liters of bottled water** ready **per person.** This serves not only to keep you hydrated, but also for makeshift personal hygiene. Just buy an extra pack of your favorite drinks (soft drinks, juices), a few packs of water also fit under the bed.

30 liters of water per person

❑ Because toilet flushing also stops working during a blackout, apartment buildings have to be evacuated after just a few days in the German *Blackout* series because of the risk of epidemics. A **camping toilet** can provide temporary relief here, either with appropriate chemicals – or airtight garbage bags.

Camping toilet

❑ In *The Book of Eli,* **wet wipes** are an expensive luxury item for a reason: they are a good temporary substitute for daily hygiene. Store a few packs of them to be able to save scarce drinking water in case of emergency without giving up the daily "shower".

Wet wipes

❑ When the water finally runs again after a long time, it may not yet have the usual drinking water quality. It is better not to rely solely on moss as a filter, as in *Radioflash.* Instead, a **water filter** for domestic use can increase food safety. For consumption, water should be boiled beforehand, especially if instructed to do so by the authorities (see below for boilers).

Water filter

❑ Supermarket shelves are more stocked than ever these days, but it's not just during a blackout that supply chains can be briefly disrupted. Like Jeevan from *Station Eleven,* stock up on **emergency food** for all household members to at least be able to sit out a crisis for some time – maybe not for three months, but at least for **10 days**. In the post-apocalyptic world *of Tribes of Europa*, people are happy to have a few canned goods left over from modern times; they are often good for (somewhat) longer than printed on them, even if not 45 years as in the series. Accordingly, everything is allowed that keeps longer **without refrigeration**, tastes good and is good for you (consider intolerances!). Think also of special food for infants and those in need of care, as well as the food for your pets.

Food stock for 10 days minimum

❑ Stockpiling tip: Like Will Smith's character in *I Am Legend*, use up foods with short best-before dates regularly in everyday life and always sort products with the longest shelf life in the back of the pantry.

Roll supplies

❑ Another tip: You should not eat too much leftover meat and ice cream during a blackout for fear that your food from the fridge and freezer will spoil. The cops of *Brooklyn Nine-Nine* only survive this because of almost superhuman digestive abilities. Don't risk food poisoning and only consume what you would otherwise eat. Anything that cannot be adequately refrigerated or properly prepared must be littered.

Dispose defrosted or unrefrigerated food

❑ So that you don't have to rely on the rampant dealer next door in case of illness, as in *Sløborn*, you should have a well-maintained **medicine cabinet** at home with painkillers, antipyretics and diarrhea remedies, as well as a **first-aid kit.** Remember your **prescription medications**, because in what feels like every blackout movie (such as *World War Z*), the asthma inhaler gets lost at the wrong moment.

Home pharmacy, first aid kit, prescriptions

❑ *Seattle Firefighters* battle carbon monoxide poisoning (fireplaces in poorly ventilated spaces) and the threat of explosions (candles in buildings with damaged gas lines). Therefore, to heat water and food, it is better to rely on **dry fuels** that do not produce toxic gases and innovative solutions such as **heating bags** that safely heat food through a chemical reaction with water. Light is better not made with fire, but with flashlights (see below).

Makeshift cooker: dry fuels or flameless heater bags

❑ Because emergency calls cannot be made easily during a long-lasting area-wide blackout and the fire department will be overwhelmed, one should have a **fire extinguisher, fire blanket** and, of course, **smoke detectors** in the household, preferably also a **hose** and **bucket.** Those who absolutely must use a (certified!) **paraffin oil heater** or **gas cooker** should definitely follow the **safety instructions,** especially regular extensive ventilation, and official regulation. Fuels must be properly stored so that they do not cause a disaster themselves. Due to the particular dangers (risk of fatal carbon monox-

Fire protection, safe heater, warm clothes

ide poisoning, fire source) and unfamiliar handling, emergency stoves of any kind should be the very last resort – rather make do with warm **clothing, pocket warmers, blankets** and a hot drink – or a warming fellow human.

❏ Without a **radio set,** the power failure-stricken people would be completely lost, as in *The Fog, The Happening* and *Under the Dome,* because without a radio set, neither news nor official emergency information can be received. Keep enough batteries on hand to stay informed for at least two weeks. Combination devices that can also be charged with an integrated solar cell or crank are ideal. Don't rely on rumors and meddlers, who only make things worse in *Into the Forest* with their conspiracy theories. Insider tip: In *A Quiet Place: Part II,* the radio even serves to efficiently fight the extremely ear-sensitive alien monsters in the grand finale, so it's definitely worth having one.

Radio
with batteries or
solar panel

❏ In *Pastewka, Peppa Pig* and *Desperate Housewives,* the protagonists get injured because they have trouble finding their way around in the dark at home during the blackout. It's not for nothing that the first order of business in most blackout movies and show episodes is to find a **flashlight.** Every member of the household should have one of these, along with **spare batteries.**

Flashlights
(one per person)
with batteries

❏ Blackout movies like *The Trigger Effect* show that during a power outage, card payments also

Cash

fail. If you don't want to pay with your wedding ring or get ripped off in any other way, always keep a small **cash reserve** at home so that you can still buy the bare essentials without a credit card.

☐ Anyone who urgently depends on their vehicle should be aware that in the event of a power outage, the pumps at gas stations will no longer work. In apocalyptic scenarios like *How It Ends*, the **spare gas can** proves to be a last resort. However, be aware of the maximum amounts allowed to be carried in the car. Tip: Fill up when the tank is still **half full.**

Spare gas can, full tank

☐ In *High School Musical – The Musical – The Series*, the teenagers know that you can only write to your parents via smartphone if you still have **battery power,** and after a short time they are already fighting over a **power bank.** It's only of any use if you regularly discharge it and recharge it directly. It can also be used to keep other important devices operational, such as **walkie talkies** for home use, with which you can still communicate locally wirelessly when the mobile network is long gone – just like the survival turtle doves in the zombie apocalypse of *#Alive*.

Power bank, walkie talkies

☐ Tip: To make sure you can reach your loved ones from another device, **write down the most important cell phone and landline numbers,** the 'old-fashioned' way, in a small address book – along with the phone numbers and addresses of your city hall, local fire department and nearest

Printed address book

police station. You may also know a few numbers by heart, even the eight-year-old girl from *Station Eleven* can manage that.

☐ Did you know that your access to the landline is likely to fail immediately in the event of a power outage? In the German TV series *Blackout,* even nuclear power plants can no longer make phone calls. This is because telephone calls are nowadays made almost everywhere via the Internet ("Voice over IP"). If the power, and thus routers, fail, you can no longer get online, even though the switchboards have been working for some time. A small UPS ("uninterruptible power supply") or a **battery with wall power socket** can serve as a bridging device for the first few hours. If you are absolutely dependent on constant telephone accessibility for professional reasons (like the U.S. president in *Y – The Last Man*) or for private reasons (like the impostor Eugene in *The Walking Dead*), investing in a simple **satellite telephone** with a prepaid card can make sense. Note: With some providers, the credit expires after a short time.

UPS or power station, satellite phone

☐ If you are absolutely dependent on electricity, for example because you have family members at home with high care needs (e.g. home respirators as in *Chicago Fire*), the purchase of an emergency power supply must be considered. Noisy and exhaust-intensive fuel generators are at best something for rural homeowners with large yards. More practical are portable **power**

Emergency power supply

stations with solar panels, which allow a certain independence in *Y – The Last Man.*

☐ Not all movie and TV characters think, as in *How It Ends,* that it might become necessary to leave home quickly in an emergency situation. A prepared **escape backpack** should contain (in addition to the already named most necessary things for at least two days) protective clothing including rubber boots, a pocket knife and respiratory masks as well as **important documents** in the original (certificates) or if necessary as a certified copy (policies, notices, certificates, powers of attorney, IDs, vaccination certificate).

Emergency backpack with documents

☐ Tip: It's best to keep your waterproof **document folder** in an easily accessible place where you can quickly grab it when you need it. There is also room for the most important family photos (if necessary on a CD or memory card).

Easy accessible documents and data backup

☐ Do it better than the movie and TV characters who are regularly taken completely by surprise by the blackout: Have you talked to your family and friends about what you want to do in the event of a blackout? Have you agreed on which trusted neighbors and acquaintances to ask for help or refuge from in an emergency, and where to meet in case of an emergency? Have you developed an **emergency plan** that you update regularly? Also talk to your children about the topic in an age-appropriate way: *Max* and his dog *Flocke* from the German Federal Office of Civil Protection and Disaster Assistance (BBK), for example, know their way around

Emergency plan

and speak many different languages. For the
US, check ready.gov/kids

- ❏ Another important tip: If the zombies or a tornado announce themselves and thus the blackout threatens, the sirens wail in *#Alive* and *Superstore*. In Germany, a one-minute rising and
falling wail sounds in dangerous situations. In
this case, the rule is to turn on the radio and
wait for information. When the danger has
passed, this is signaled by a one-minute continuous tone in Germany. Find out what the warning signals apply in your country.
Know siren signals

- ❏ Note: In the event of a blackout, **turn off all
appliances (especially the stove and gas).** When
power is restored, appliances should only be
turned back on gradually to prevent overloading the grid and causing another outage.
*Turn off all
appliances*

LITERATURE

ACHERMANN, HANS (2018): „Eine sichere Stromversorgung ist keine Selbstverständlichkeit", in SCHIPS, BERND; BORNER, SILVIO (eds.): *Versorgungssicherheit. Vom politischen Kurzschluss zum Blackout.* Basel: Carnot-Cournot, pp. 32–77.

ACKERMANN, ELLIOT; STAVRIDIS, JAMES (2021): *2034 – A novel of the next world war.* New York: Penguin Books.

AKREMI, LEILA (2011): *Kommunikative Konstruktion von Zukunftsängsten.* Wiesbaden: Springer.

BAHR, PETRA (2001): „„Das Ende ist da'. Anmerkungen zu einer heiklen Sprechpraxis an der Zeitenwende", in FRÖLICH, MARGRIT; MIDDEL, REINHARD; VISARIUS, KARSTEN (eds.): *Nach dem Ende. Auflösung und Untergänge im Kino an der Jahrtausendwende.* Marburg: Schüren, pp. 9–23.

BECK, ULRICH ([1986]2020): *Risikogesellschaft. Auf dem Weg in eine andere Moderne.* Frankfurt am Main: Suhrkamp.

BECK, ULRICH (2007): *Weltrisikogesellschaft. Auf der Suche nach der verlorenen Sicherheit.* Frankfurt: Suhrkamp.

BECK, ULRICH (2017): *Weltrisiko. Die Metamorphose der Welt.* Frankfurt: Suhrkamp.

BERGER, PETER L.; LUCKMANN, THOMAS (1995): *Modernität, Pluralismus und Sinnkrise. Die Orientierung des modernen Menschen.* Gütersloh: Bertelsmann-Stiftung.

BBK (Bundesamt für Bevölkerungsschutz und Katastrophenhilfe) (2022): „Strategie zur Stärkung der Resilienz gegenüber Katastrophen", bbk.bund.de/DE /Themen/Nationale-Kontaktstelle-Sendai-Rahmenwerk/Resilienzstrategie/resilienz-strategie_node.html, accessed on February 23rd, 2022.

BONß, WOLFGANG (1995): *Vom Risiko. Unsicherheit und Ungewissheit in der Moderne*. Hamburg: Hamburger Edition.

BORNER, SILVIO; SCHIPS, BERND (2018): „Wie sicher ist unsere Stromversorgung wirklich?", in SCHIPS, BERND; BORNER, SILVIO (eds.): *Versorgungssicherheit. Vom politischen Kurzschluss zum Blackout*. Basel: Carnot-Cournot, pp. 13–31.

ELSBERG, MARC ([2012]2017): *Blackout – Tomorrow will be too late*, London: Black Swan.

ESPOSITO, ELENA (2014): *Die Fiktion der wahrscheinlichen Realität*. Frankfurt am Main: Suhrkamp.

FUKUYAMA, FRANCIS (1992): *The end of history and the last man*. New York: Free Press.

GOODMAN, NELSON (2007): *Weisen der Welterzeugung*. Frankfurt am Main: Suhrkamp.

GROÏS, BORIS (2000): *Unter Verdacht. Eine Phänomenologie der Medien*. München: Hanser.

GROSS, LARRY; MORGAN, MICHAEL (1985): „Television and Enculturation", in DOMINICK, JOSEPH R.; FLETCHER, JAMES E. (eds.): *Broadcasting Research Methods*. Boston: Allyn and Bacon, pp. 221–234.

HARTLEY, JOHN (2014): *Uses of television*. London/New York: Routledge.

HAWKING, STEPHEN (2020): *Kurze Antworten auf große Fragen.* London: Klett-Cotta.

HEINBERG, RICHARD (2009): *Blackout. Coal, climate and the last energy crisis.* Gabriola Island: New Society Publishers.

HICKETHIER, KNUT (1994): „Die Fernsehserie und das Serielle des Programms", in GIESENFELD, GÜNTER (eds.): *Endlose Geschichten. Serialität in den Medien.* Hildesheim: Olms, pp. 55–71.

HICKETHIER, KNUT (2008): „Fernsehen, Rituale und Subjektkonstitutionen. Ein Kapitel Fernsehtheorie", in FAHLENBRACH, KATHRIN; BRÜCK, INGRID; BARTSCH, ANNE (eds.): *Medienrituale. Rituelle Performanz in Film, Fernsehen und Neuen Medien.* Wiesbaden: VS Verlag für Sozialwissenschaften, pp. 47–58.

HORN, EVA (2014): *Zukunft als Katastrophe.* Frankfurt am Main: S. Fischer.

KARSTEN, ANDREAS H. (2020): „Stromausfall", in VOßSCHMIDT, STEFAN; KARSTEN, ANDREAS (eds.): *Resilienz und Kritische Infrastrukturen. Aufrechterhaltung von Versorgungstrukturen im Krisenfall.* Stuttgart: Kohlhammer Verlag, pp. 314–320.

KEANE, STEPHEN (2006): *Disaster movies. The cinema of catastrophe.* London: Wallflower Press.

KEPPLER, ANGELA (2006): *Mediale Gegenwart. Eine Theorie des Fernsehens am Beispiel der Darstellung von Gewalt.* Frankfurt am Main: Suhrkamp.

KIRCHMANN, KAY (2006): „Philosophie der Möglichkeiten. Das Fernsehen als konjunktivisches Erzählmedium" in FAHLE, OLIVER; ENGELL,

LORENZ (eds.): *Philosophie des Fernsehens*. München: Fink, pp. 157–172.

KLEINER, MARCUS S. (2013): „Apocalypse (Not) Now? Performative Bildungsprozesse in Populären Medienkulturen – am Beispiel der US-amerikanischen Fernseh-Serie ‚The Walking Dead'" in KLEINER, MARCUS S.; WILKE, THOMAS (eds.): *Performativität und Medialität populärer Kulturen. Theorien, Ästhetiken, Praktiken*. Wiesbaden: Springer VS, pp. 225–252.

KRAH, HANS (2004): *Weltuntergangsszenarien und Zukunftsentwürfe. Narrationen vom „Ende" in Literatur und Film 1945 – 1990*. Kiel: Ludwig.

LILLEMOSE, JACOB (2021): „Was kommt nach dem Ende der Welt? Anmerkungen zu postapokalyptischen Bildwelten in Katastrophenfilmen", in PLAPPERT, STEFANIE (ed.): *Katastrophe – Was kommt nach dem Ende?* Frankfurt am Main: DFF, pp. 11–16.

LUHMANN, NIKLAS (1987): „Tautologie und Paradoxie in den Selbstbeschreibungen der modernen Gesellschaft", in *Zeitschrift für Soziologie* 16(3), pp. 161–174.

LUHMANN, NIKLAS (1991): *Soziologie des Risikos*. Berlin: de Gruyter.

LUHMANN, NIKLAS (1996): *Die Realität der Massenmedien*. Berlin: VS Verlag für Sozialwissenschaften.

MAIKÄMPER, MORITZ; KRÄMER, STEFFEN; PÄTSCH, CAROLIN; PETERSEN, CHRISTER; ROTT, BODO; RUKSCHCIO, BELINDA; WEIDNER, SILKE (2015): *Von Science-Fiction-Städten lernen. Szenarien für die Stadtplanung. Ein Projekt des Forschungsprogramms „Experimenteller*

Wohnungs- und Städtebau" des Bundesministeriums für Umwelt, Naturschutz, Bau und Reaktorsicherheit. Bonn: Bundesamt für Bauwesen und Raumordnung.

MAYER, JULIA ET AL. (2017): *Treibstoffversorgung bei Stromausfall. Empfehlung für Zivil- und Katastrophenschutzbehörden.* Bonn: Bundesamt für Bevölkerungsschutz und Katastrophenhilfe.

NASSEHI, ARMIN (2021): *Unbehagen. Theorie der überforderten Gesellschaft.* München: C. H. Beck.

NEWIAK, DENIS (2021): *It's all been there before. What we can learn about the coronavirus from pandemic movies.* Stuttgart: ibidem.

NEWIAK, DENIS (2022a): *Die Einsamkeiten der Moderne. Eine Theorie der Modernisierung als Zeitalter der Vereinsamung.* Wiesbaden: Springer VS.

NEWIAK, DENIS (2022b): „How Television Produces Invisible Communities in an Age of Loneliness. A Detailed Look at 13 Reasons Why" in BENKO, STEVEN (ed.): *Better Living With TV. Contemporary TV and Moral Identity Formation.* Lanham/Boulder/New York/London: Lexington Books, pp. 227–254.

PAULITZ, HENRIK (2021): „Die Stromversorgung ist massiv gefährdet" in *Telepolis* vom 21. Januar 2021, heise.de/tp/features/Die-Stromversorgung-ist-massiv-gefaehrdet-5030116.html

PETERMANN, THOMAS; BRADKE, HARALD; LÜLLMANN, ARNE; POETZSCH, MAIK; RIEHM, ULRICH (2011): *What happens during a blackout: Consequences of a prolonged and wide-*

ranging power outage. Office of Technology Assessment at the German Bundestag (TAB).

PITZKE, MARC (2007): „New Yorks dunkelste Nacht" in *Der Spiegel,* July 13th, 2007, spiegel.de/panorama/zeitgeschichte/blackout-von-1977-new-yorks-dunkelstenacht-a-493609.html

RIES, REINHARD; BRÜCKMANN, MICHAEL; FESKE, LEONHARD (2012): „Stromausfall – Herausforderung für die Feuerwehr" in GERHOLD, LARS; SCHILLER, JOCHEN (eds.): *Perspektiven der Sicherheitsforschung. Beiträge aus dem Forschungsforum Öffentliche Sicherheit.* Frankfurt: Peter Lang, pp. 193–204.

SCHNEIDER, PETER (2018): „Stromversorgung: Ein gravierendes sicherheitspolitisches Problem?", in SCHIPS, BERND; BORNER, SILVIO (eds.): *Versorgungssicherheit. Vom politischen Kurzschluss zum Blackout.* Basel: Carnot-Cournot, pp. 151–167.

STEINBORN, ANKE; NEWIAK, DENIS (2020): „Wahrscheinliche' Zukünfte: Urbanes Leben mit Science-Fiction neu gedacht" in STEINBORN, ANKE; NEWIAK, DENIS (eds.): *Urbane Zukünfte im Science-Fiction-Film. Was wir vom Kino für die Stadt von morgen lernen können.* Berlin: Springer Spektrum, pp. 1–10.

STICHER, BIRGITTA; BOEHME, KARL; GEIßLER, SARAH (2010): „Als das Münsterland plötzlich dunkel wurde. Ein regional begrenzter Stromausfall im Jahr 2005 und dessen Bedeutung für Deutschland" in *CD Sicherheitsmanagement,* Jg. 24(2), pp. 30–40.

WARREN, MATTHEW (2018): *Black out: how is energy-rich Australia running out of electricity?* South Melbourne: Affirm Press.

WELZL, NORBERT (2010): „Black Out – Sind Sie ausreichend vorbereitet?" in *CD Sicherheitsmanagement*, Jg. 24(2), pp. 18–29.

ŽIŽEK, SLAVOJ (2011): *Living in the end times.* London: Verso.

DISCUSSED FILMS AND TV SHOWS

Motion Pictures

10 Cloverfield Lane (USA 2016)

14 Hours (USA 2005)

380.000 Volt – Der Große Stromausfall (D 2010)

Awake (USA 2021)

Bird Box (USA 2018)

Blackout (USA 2007)

Blackout (USA 2008)

Blackout – Terror Just Hit the Lights (USA 2011)

Blade Runner Black Out 2022 (USA/JP 2017)

Blade Runner (USA/HK 1982)

The Book of Eli (USA 2010)

Cell (USA 2017)

Close Encounters of the Third Kind (USA 1977)

Cloverfield (USA 2008)

The Darkest Hour (USA 2011)

Dawn of the Dead (USA 2004)

Dawn of the Planet of the Apes (USA 2014)

Devil (USA 2010)

Fin (S 2012)

The Fog (USA 1980)

Into the Forest (CA 2015)

The Happening (USA/IN/FR 2008)

How It Ends (USA 2018)

I Am Legend (USA 2007)

Die kommenden Tage (D 2010)

Live Free or Die Hard (USA 2007)

Outbreak (USA 1995)

The Purge (USA 2013)

The Quiet Earth (NZ 1985)

Radioflash (USA 2019)

#Saraitda (KR 2020)

The Rain (DK 2018–2020)

Then There Was (USA 2014)

Transcendence (USA 2014)

The Trigger Effect (USA 1996)

War of the Worlds (USA 2005)

The Wolf Hour (USA 2019)

World War Z (USA 2013)

Yesterday (UK 2019)

TV Shows

All of Us Are Dead (KR 2022)

Avanpost ("The Blackout", RU 2020)

The Big Bang Theory (USA 2007–2019): "The Friendship Contraction (S05E15)

Black Summer (USA 2019–)

Blackout (D 2021–)

Black-Out (BE 2020–2021)

Bones (USA 2005–2017): "The Blackout In The Blizzard" (S06E16)

Broen (DK) / *Bron* (SE) (DK/S/D 2011–2018): "Episode 1" (S01E01)

Brooklyn Nine-Nine (USA 2013–): "Lights Out" (S07E13)

Bugs (UK 1995–1999): "Blackout" (S02E05)

Chicago Fire (USA 2012–): "Tonight's The Night" (S02E13)

Code Black (USA 2015–2017): "Exodus" (S02E11)

Cosby (USA 1996–2000): "Lucas Apocalypse" (S04E04)

Dark (D 2017–2020)

Desperate Housewives (USA 2004–2012): "God, That's Good" (S03E19)

Designated Survivor (USA 2016–2019): "In the Dark" (S02E14)

Edel und Starck (D 2002–2005): "Do it yourself" (S03E01)

L'Effondrement (FR 2019)

Emergency Room (USA 1994–2009): "Blackout" (S14E07)

Family Matters (USA 1989–1998): "Christmas Is Where The Heart Is" (S05E11)

Fear the Walking Dead (USA 2015–): "The Dog" (S01E03)

Fear the Walking Dead: Flight 462 (USA 2015–2016)

The Flash (USA 2015–): "Power Outage" (S01E07)

Friends (USA 1994–2004): "The One With The Blackout" (S01E07)

Grey's Anatomy (USA 2005–): "Bring the Pain" (S02E05), "Perfect Storm" (S09E24), "Blowin' in the Wind" (S15E08), "Shelter from the Storm" (S15E09)

The Good Doctor (USA 2017–):
"Decrypt" (S04E10)

Growing Pains (USA 1985–1992):
"The Wrath of Con Ed" (S07E22)

*High School Musical – The
Musical – The Series* (USA 2019–):
"The Storm" (S02E04)

Into the Night (BE 2020–)

*Lois & Clark: The New
Adventures of Superman* (USA
1993–1997): "Operation
Blackout" (S02E06)

Malcolm in the Middle (USA
2000–2006): "Blackout" (S07E07)

Married… With Children (USA
1987–1997): "You Better Shop
Around" (S05E21/22)

The Mist (USA 2017)

Monk (USA 2002–2009):
"Mr. Monk And The Blackout"
(S03E03)

The Newsroom (USA 2012–2014)

Pastewka (D 2005–2014, 2018–
2020): "Das Gewitter" (S05E08)

Peppa Pig (USA 2004–): "The
Powercut" (S02E47)

The Purge (USA 2018–2019)

The Rain (DK 2018–2020)

Revolution (USA 2012–2014)

The Simpsons (USA 1989–):
"Poppa's Got a Brand New
Badge" (S13E22)

Sløborn (D 2020–)

The Society (USA 2019)

The Stand (USA 2020–2021)

Station 19 (USA 2018–):
"The Dark Night" (S02E13)

Station Eleven (USA 2022)

Superstore (USA 2015–2021):
"Tornado" (S02E22)

Sweet Home (KR 2020)

Tribes of Europa (D 2021–)

Under the Dome (USA 2013–
2015)

Unité 42 („Unit 42", B 2017–):
"Reboot" (S01E10)

The Walking Dead (USA 2010–
2022)

The Walking Dead: World Beyond
(USA 2020–2021)

War of the Worlds (USA/FR 2019)

Wayward Pines (USA 2015–2016):
"Cycle" (S01E10)

White Collar (USA 2009–2014):
"Power Play" (S02E15)

Y – The Last Man (USA 2021)

DR. DENIS NEWIAK
(born 1988 in Potsdam) studied European Media Studies at the University of Potsdam and Film Studies at the Free University of Berlin. He received his doctorate from the Brandenburg University of Technology Cottbus-Senftenberg on expressions of loneliness in film and television and a theory of modernity as an age of increasing loneliness. He conducts research on the community-creating functions of television series under late-modern living conditions as well as on the knowledge of the future contained in science fiction films, especially with regard to modern catastrophic potentials such as extreme weather events and artificial intelligence. He completed several extended research stays at the Library of Congress in Washington, D. C., and teaches management and leadership techniques in addition to journalism and media theory at the university. He is a volunteer paramedic with the German Lifesaving Society (DLRG) and a licensed competitive sports coach for ballroom dancing with the German Olympic Sports Confederation (DOSB).